We are the Angels

We are the Angels

Healing Our Past, Present, and Future with
THE LORDS OF KARMA

Diane Stein

THE CROSSING PRESS
FREEDOM, CALIFORNIA

Cover and Interior design by Tara M. Eoff
Photo © 1997 Anselm Spring/The Image Bank
Illustrations by Ian/Everard
Printed in U.S.A.

For information on bulk purchases or group discounts for this and other Crossing Press titles, please contact our Special Sales Manager at 800-777-1048.

Visit our Web site on the Internet: www.crossingpress.com.

Library of Congress Cataloging-in-Publication Data

Stein, Diane, 1948-
We are the angels: healing our past, present, and future with the Lords of Karma / Stein.
p. cm.
ISBN 0-89594-878-8 (pbk.)
1. Karma--Miscellanea. 2. Spiritual healing--Miscellanea.
3. Angels--Miscellanea. 4. Goddess religion. I. Title.
BF1045.K37S74 1997
291.2'2--dc21 97-23847
CIP

I would like to thank Karen Silverman for encouraging these energy explorations and for being my first and foremost guinea pig to the processes. Her superb psychic abilities often analyzed them and told me what it was that I had done. Thanks to Corinne Nichols who tried them next, Robyn Zimmerman for telling me who Nada is, and to Dorothy Byrne who wanted more.

Thanks also to Josh Silverman, five years old, for informing me that I was leaving a "temple" out of the Energy Balancing Process, and thereby discovering the I-Am Template (which he also named). Thanks to his mother Karen for allowing him to be the first child to experience the Lords of Karma and Energy Balancing.

Special thanks, too, to Kali and Copper who proved that all of this can benefit dogs. Copper informed me he had already done it a few times, before I ever thought of it.

Thanks always to Elaine Gill, Karen Narita, Cyndi Barnes, Jane Lazear, and all the other wonderful folks at The Crossing Press who publish my books and who are willing to trust me with such very weird stuff.

For Sue

CONTENTS

PART I—HEALING KARMA

Karma and the Earth Changes .13
Soul Structure 23
Reincarnation 37
The Four Kinds of Karma 47
The Process of Rebirth 57
The Lords of Karma 67
Karmic Release 79
Healing Others 91

PART II—ENERGY BALANCING

Ascension and the Higher Self 103
The Energy Balancing Process 115
Energy Balancing and Core Soul Healing 125
Essence Self, Goddess Self, and Goddess 137
Follow Up 147

APPENDIX

Appendix I—Working With the Lords of Karma 155
Appendix II—The Energy Balancing Process 157

DIAGRAMS

The Kundalini Chakras 29
The Hara Line Chakras 30
The Templates and Energy Bodies 33
Hara Healing Symbols 151

PART I

Healing Karma

Karma and the Earth Changes

THE PRIMARY TENET OF WICCA IS "YOU ARE GODDESS." Whether you are a member of the Goddess Craft or not, the idea is an important one. The Earth is a Goddess, known to some as Gaia, and Goddess—a spark of divine energy by whatever name you choose to call divinity—is present in the life of every individual person, animal, or plant. Whether you call that spark of life force Goddess, God, Buddha, Christ, Allah, the Universe, All-That-Is, or some other name, the concept is the same. Without that spark of divinity, nothing lives. With it, the Earth and all her inhabitants (human and otherwise) are living Be-ings and a part of the one life of the planet and universe. All life is one. I choose to call that life force Goddess—replace that name with whatever name you wish. Goddess is the Earth, but she is also all who live upon the Earth and carry her spark of life force.

We are each a part of the Earth, and the Earth changes are manifesting first and foremost in those of us who are her life force. They are not limited only to people, but are also occurring in plant and animal life, including the microscopic life we seldom stop to think about. The changes are occurring in the minerals and gases that form the physical Earth, as well as in the nonphysical levels of thought and deed in Earth's inhabitants. They are occurring far more on the nonphysical levels than they are on the evident physical ones, and are occurring far more on nonconscious than on conscious levels. When racism, for example, is changed to an understanding of equality, an honoring of all life, it is far more significant (and Earth healing) than an earthquake, though an earthquake may be physically observed and measured.

Current discussions of the Earth changes describe future cataclysms and destruction on the planet: natural and man-made disasters, landmass changes, societal and governmental breakdowns, technological failures, wars, violence, dis-eases, and other forms of chaos. The reason for these events is to create realization of what is right for the Earth and for those living on it, and to foster an eventual return to peace, ecology, freedom, and moral sanity. The predictions have come from dozens of psychics and channelers, and many have been accurate. Goddess Earth is definitely in trouble, with the first embattled seeds of needed change only now beginning to appear.

The primary evidence of the Earth changes can be seen in the changing, healing, and energy clearing of individuals. That healing and clearing is manifested primarily through karmic healing, whether people are aware of it happening or not. The increasing stress and difficulty of the past several years and the increasing intensity in everyone's life reflect the working out of this process. Whatever has not been healed in an individual's personal karma and numerous past lives is presenting itself for change with increasing insistence. Anything in one's life that is not working is totally breaking down, whether it be relationships, careers, lifestyles, behaviors, or thought patterns. No one is comfortable with the process but most lives will be happier with the end results.

The healing of the Earth that is the purpose of the Earth changes means the healing of people, Earth's population as a whole and as individuals. No group healing happens without the healing of each individual in the group. The Earth cannot heal until all who live here are healed. The karmic release and healing of the planet is what the Earth changes are. The karmic release and healing of individuals is what makes the Earth changes possible and manifests them on seen and unseen levels. The chaos we are experiencing now, on the Earth and in people, is the evidence of that incomplete release in process. Its completion will lead to the New Age of peace and well-being for everyone, every individual, country, and the Earth.

The completion of the Earth changes in individuals will also lead to happier and more stable people who know and validate their purpose in life, and who honor the purpose and life force/Goddess in all lives. It means being in relationships of all sorts that honor and respect the equality and life force of both partners. It means working at jobs and careers where people are treated humanely and honestly, have adequate hours for leisure, and are paid a living wage. It means recognizing the oneness of all life in oneself and all others, and the honoring of all races and differences. The completion of the Earth changes in people means food and shelter for all and an end to abuse, poverty, homelessness, violence, misogyny, malnutrition, lack of education, and lack of personal freedom. It means a new Earth because of the new awareness of Earth's people. Much healing still needs to be done to reach this point.

Karma in these Earth change times is the individual working out of every unresolved suffering and negative deed from every past life and from this life on Earth. Every suffering that has been experienced (given or received) remains in the individual's energy makeup until it has been resolved and released. Every suffering that resides in human (or animal) energy is a part of the suffering that is also happening to groups or nations. By healing and releasing this ongoing pain the individual is released from experiencing or committing it again, and the people of Earth collectively are also released from its recurrence. Release happens by realization, realization of the suffering and realization that such suffering cannot be tolerated or perpetuated. The Wiccan adage for this is "what you send out returns to you." It may be better known as "do unto others as you would have others do unto you." Another way of putting it may be, "the buck stops here." By releasing yourself from suffering and breaking the ongoing chain of perpetuation, the suffering ends for all.

As an example, there is the all too familiar women's issue of incest recovery. A woman who has been abused, raped, or incested goes through an often painful, very difficult recovery process. The abuse has affected her in every way—in her body (physically), in her feelings (emotionally), in her thoughts (mentally), and in her understanding of herself in relation to others and the Universe (spiritually). In her ongoing relationships she unknowingly draws to herself those who would repeat the energy of the incest by manipulating and abusing her. Through her healing process, she gains understanding of how she was harmed and the knowledge that she was not to blame. She resolves her hurt and anger in life-affirming ways. By accepting and talking about what happened to her and learning how her abuse has affected her adult life, she releases its negative effects and no longer draws abuse to herself. In her growing understanding, she decides that what happened to her will not be permitted to happen to her daughter, and she teaches her daughter self-worth and the ability to protect herself. The incest is healed in the woman and is not perpetuated in her child.

To take her healing to completion, she must release the karma of the incest from her energy bodies. To do this she asks that the incest be healed and released at its source, a source likely from a past lifetime. She asks for karmic release from her perpetrator. By understanding the incidents of abuse in her past lives and how that unhealed pattern from the past has manifested in the present for healing, she releases it totally. Now the suffering is removed completely from her energy bodies, from this life and past lives, so it will not perpetuate in her future. She will not meet her perpetrator in further lifetimes. With this karmic release and the karmic healing that goes with it, the chain of suffering is fully broken. It is no longer carried forward in her Akashic Record of incarnations, and it is no longer carried forward in her DNA. Incest is removed from her life (and lifetimes) totally. She draws positive relationships to herself and protects her daughter. One piece of suffering is removed from the planet.

When enough individuals have cleared their experience of sexual abuse in this way, such abuse will not perpetuate on Earth. The healing has therefore manifested in the woman who was incested, in her child or children, in future generations (her children's children), in the group suffering of others, and on the Earth. The Earth has changed, and a portion of the Earth changes has been accomplished.

Those who define karma as "an eye for an eye, a tooth for a tooth" are incorrect. Karma is never so easy nor so simple. It does not often mean that a person who has committed a crime in one lifetime will have the same crime done to her in the next incarnation. Negative actions do create injury to the individual's energy and a person who commits an injustice may later be required to experience a similar one to clear and learn from it. The woman who was incested, however, is less likely to have been a perpetrator in a past life than a sufferer from earlier incest. More often, karma is suffering that is not healed in the lifetime in which it happened. The injury remains in the person's aura (mental body and mind grid). For the karma to be released, the injury recurs again and again (becomes a karmic pattern) until realization and learning releases it. Once this healing happens, the suffering is finished; until the healing occurs, the suffering continues or repeats through the person's current lifetime and across the boundaries of death and rebirth.

Karma is not a punishment. It is simply an energy of pain and injury that has to be cleared and removed. The experience of suffering carries the lesson that such suffering must never be repeated—a woman who has been healed of past incest is not likely to allow the sexual abuse of anyone else in this lifetime or a future one. Suffering has purpose in human and animal life and animals also have karma. Its purpose is to teach compassion for others, and to prompt a level of spiritual growth that makes it impossible for first the individual and eventually for anyone to harm someone else or oneself. Karma is a process of learning and soul growth in which each individual learns and comes to understand the consequences of her actions and her pain. By understanding the consequences, she also learns to act in ways that bring joy instead of suffering to herself and to others. This learning is necessary and crucial. When everyone has learned this lesson there will be no further need for suffering or karma and the Earth changes will be complete.

When an individual learns this lesson in all its aspects, and heals all the damage to her energy from past trauma and pain, she is no longer required to reincarnate. She no longer suffers or causes suffering to others. In the Buddhist and Hindu traditions this is considered the ultimate goal and the only real healing. The Christian heaven is derived from the Buddhist Devachan, the Pure Land or place of grace, into which one may be born and where one can easily achieve release from rebirth. Life contains suffering because it is only in the body that old hurts resurface to be healed. They are not healed in the between-life state or anywhere else but in incarnation in a body. When all suffering is released and healed from one's energy field, and the person has the realization of the oneness of all life and compassion for all, she no longer has to reincarnate or continue to experience pain.

This is exactly what is occurring in the Earth changes for both individuals and the planet. We have reached a place where the suffering in people and the Earth must be released if the planet and people are to survive and continue. People are experiencing suffering in intensive ways at this time because all past pain that has not yet been healed is surfacing for completion. Such pain in people is as devastating and overwhelming as the cataclysms and disasters on the planet, and may also be entwined with Earth cataclysms. Where the disasters on the planet have the purpose of forcing governments and nations to make changes that honor the life force in individuals and the Earth, the suffering in people has the purpose of forcing individuals to heal the harm and damage of all their lifetimes. In both cases, the disasters often seem impossible to deal with. In both cases, they involve an energy clearing, a releasing and sometimes reliving of the energy of pain to remove it from the aura so it never has to be relived again. Those people unable to face the clearing are now leaving the planet, many of them dying young.

We are not alone in our healing. The tools are available to make karmic release and clearing simple, gentle, and accessible to anyone. As a major part of the Earth changes, we are also in a time of karmic dispensation, possibly for the first time since Earth was formed. The members of the angelic realm that guide and direct human and animal karma are now willing to work with us in every way to heal suffering and prevent it from returning—either to individual people or to the planet. This energy of clearing and core soul healing is the most exciting facet of the Earth changes, and certainly the most important and crucial. As people heal, the Earth heals. We are the Earth, the life force of the Goddess, we are Goddess.

The focus of this book is in teaching these tools. They are simple but extremely powerful. They involve working with the Lords of Karma (call them Angels of Karma, if you wish) to remove suffering and energy obstructions from your life and past lives. By healing the present and past you remove suffering, pain, and trauma from your future. The techniques involve healing the damage of past suffering from all energy levels, from all the unseen energy bodies that are the primary parts of human anatomy and life. This karmic release and core soul repair and clearing result in comprehensive healing that cannot be achieved by working only at the physical/emotional levels. The results are not aimed at the physical body but can frequently achieve physical healing. They always manifest as freedom from suffering, greater peace of mind, positive self-image and empowerment, and infinitely more joy in living. Follow the techniques carefully, with thanks and respect for the gift we have been given.

The next chapter offers a basic background in soul structure to explain the processes of karmic release and energy balancing that comprise this book.

Soul Structure

THE MAKEUP OF HUMAN OR ANIMAL ENERGY IS anything but simple. Most healers are aware of the seven kundalini chakras and the four aura bodies, but these are just the beginning of a complex and highly fascinating structure. Our physical bodies are the tip of a very large iceberg; perhaps 95% of our being is unseen, unmapped, and unknown. The material that follows is an attempt to define some of that unknown anatomy, as far as I have a rudimentary understanding of it. Where most healers emphasize the chakras, they are subordinate in the karmic healing process to the aura bodies and the templates that connect the aura bodies. I will discuss the kundalini and hara line chakras only briefly and in conjunction with their operating bodies. A more complete definition of the chakras and hara line may be found in my book *Psychic Healing with Spirit Guides and Angels*.

The etheric, emotional, mental, and spiritual bodies that are closest to the dense physical body are known to most healers. These are highly important to human and animal daily life and functioning, but are also highly important as connecting interfaces to the upper octaves of outer aura body layers. Likewise, earthplane consciousness is vital for incarnated Earth life, but there are other vital levels of soul consciousness that are less available to daily awareness. These outer personality "selves" are connected and conjoined to the outer aura bodies. Bringing them into the four closest-to-physical energy layers and into conscious awareness has profound implications for spiritual growth and comprehensive karmic healing.

Etheric Body

Beginning at the level closest to the physical body, the first energy layer is the *Etheric Body*. This aura layer contains an energy twin of the physical body known as the Etheric Double. What happens in the physical body happens first in the etheric body, and the Etheric Double is the preverbal infant-self awareness. Healing that affects the etheric level manifests changes in physical health and the physical body. The kundalini chakras are located on the etheric body, and the Ka Template connects the physical body to the etheric. The root chakra on the kundalini energy line connects with the perineum chakra on the hara line, thereby also connecting the etheric body to the next energy level.

The seven kundalini chakras are the most familiar part of energy anatomy. In humans they run in a vertical line down the front and back of the body along the spinal column. I will run through them quickly. The *root chakra*, located at the tailbone, denotes life force energy, physical identity, and survival. Its color is red, and it is the first stepped-down outlet for the energy and blueprint of the etheric body. The *belly chakra*, located below the navel, regulates creativity, sexuality, and fertility. It is described as orange in color. It is the second stepped-down transformer for the energy of the etheric level. The third chakra, placed between the lowest ribs, is the *solar plexus*. Its color is yellow; it is the third and final stepped-down outlet for the etheric. It regulates the conscious mind, rational thought processes, and psychic perception.

Next is the *heart chakra*, found at the center of the breastbone, denoted by the colors green or pink. The heart chakra brings in the downwardly transformed energy of the astral/emotional body, and connects to the hara line/emotional body through the hara line's thymus chakra just above it. The Astral Twin enters at this pair of etheric and emotional body chakras. This is the center for compassion and universal love, for feeling oneself connected to all others. The light blue *throat chakra*, at the physical throat, is the first highly stepped-down outlet of the spiritual body. This chakra regulates one's ability to express truth, artistic creation, and to receive psychic speech (empathy). It is the most complex of the chakras, because it receives consciousness of the personality "selves" and contains a complete blueprint of the physical, emotional, mental, and spiritual bodies.

The next spiritual body chakra is the *third eye*, located at the center of the forehead above the physical eyes and denoted by the color indigo. The third eye regulates psychic vision, telepathy, and clairvoyance. It is also the stepped-down transformer connection to the personal mind grid, the Earth mind grid (collective planetary consciousness), and the universal mind grid (galactic or universal consciousness). Karmic clearing and release occur at this level, to move through the four lower bodies. The third spiritual body chakra at the top of the head (the *crown*) is the final kundalini chakra. This is usually described as violet, and is the seat of beyond-physical consciousness and spirituality. All core soul healing work involving energy balancing, template clearing, and DNA healing, etc., enters the nearer-to-physical energy system through this chakra. The very stepped-down energies of the Essence Self and Oversoul are received at this level, though both are far away from daily consciousness.

These are the kundalini chakras, but mention must be made here of the backs of the chakras. These are as operative as the chakras on the front of the body and are also plug-in receivers for outer body energy. The back of the heart chakra in particular is the place where the Astral Twin merges into the Etheric Double, where the Higher Self merges into the Astral Twin, where the Essence Self/Star Self merges into the Higher Self, and where the Oversoul/Goddess Self merges her energy into the Essence Self. One's personal Goddess connects here also. More information on these energy "selves" follows. These back of the heart chakra connections comprise the Silver Cord.

Emotional/Astral Body

After the etheric body, the next energy level is the *Emotional Body*, with its connection to the outer energy level of the astral plane and the Astral Twin. The emotional body contains the hara line and hara line chakras, which connect to the etheric body/kundalini line directly at the perineum/root, thymus chakra/heart, and transpersonal point/crown. The Etheric Template connects the etheric body to the emotional/astral body and connects the thymus and heart. There are thirteen hara chakras on the emotional body, briefly described as follows.

The *transpersonal point* or Soul Star is located above the crown. Its color is clear, and the center brings outer body life force energy in to power the nearer-to-physical energy system. A pair of *vision chakras* behind the eyes is next. These chakras are silver in color, and with them the eyes may be used as lasers in psychic healing. The *causal body chakra* follows, at the base of the skull. The color is either a bright red-violet or silvery blue. This is the center for channeling and manifesting. Our access to the Higher Self is through the causal body and third eye (kundalini) chakras. The Higher Self is received at the throat, and it connects with the physical through the Astral Twin at the back of the heart chakra.

The hara line *thymus chakra*, placed high on the breastbone just above the kundalini heart, is the major connection between hara and kundalini energy bodies. Access to the astral plane beyond the emotional body and the childlike Astral Twin is through this pair of connected chakras. The thymus chakra's color is aqua; it releases the emotions and also protects the physical immune system. Next is the *diaphragm chakra*, located between and beyond the kundalini solar plexus and heart chakras. The diaphragm color is lime green and its purpose is hara line detoxification and emotional change. Below the navel, between and beyond the kundalini root and belly chakras, is the *hara chakra*. Its color is orange-brown or gold, and its function is the manifesting of one's life purpose. The *perineum chakra*, placed between anus and vagina on the nonphysical emotional level, is maroon in color and its function is transcendence of the physical. The etheric and emotional bodies are also joined at this center.

Two smaller pairs of chakras are next on the hara line. The first pair is called the *movement chakras*. Placed behind the knees they aid one's movement forward on her life path. Their color is forest green or tan. A pair of brown *grounding chakras* is located at the bottoms of the feet. Their purpose is the spirit's connection to the physical incarnation. The last hara chakra is the *Earth chakra* or Earth Star, below the feet. The color is shiny black, and this chakra's purpose is to stabilize one's connection to the planet.

The emotional body contains access to the astral plane, the place of soul travel to outer realms. It also houses the Astral Twin. This free spirit child-self (as opposed to the infant-self of the Etheric Double) contains a developed awareness that may or may not be available to the conscious mind. She is gentle, vulnerable, and inquisitive, easily hurt and easily energy-damaged. She may be the origin of the concept of the "inner child." When fully healed of past damage, the Astral Twin will merge with the Etheric Double, thereby strengthening both and becoming a joyful part of conscious spiritual awareness. Another template, the Ketheric Template, connects the emotional body to the mental body, as well as connecting the kundalini third eye with the hara line causal body chakras.

DIAGRAM 1. THE KUNDALINI CHAKRAS
Etheric Body

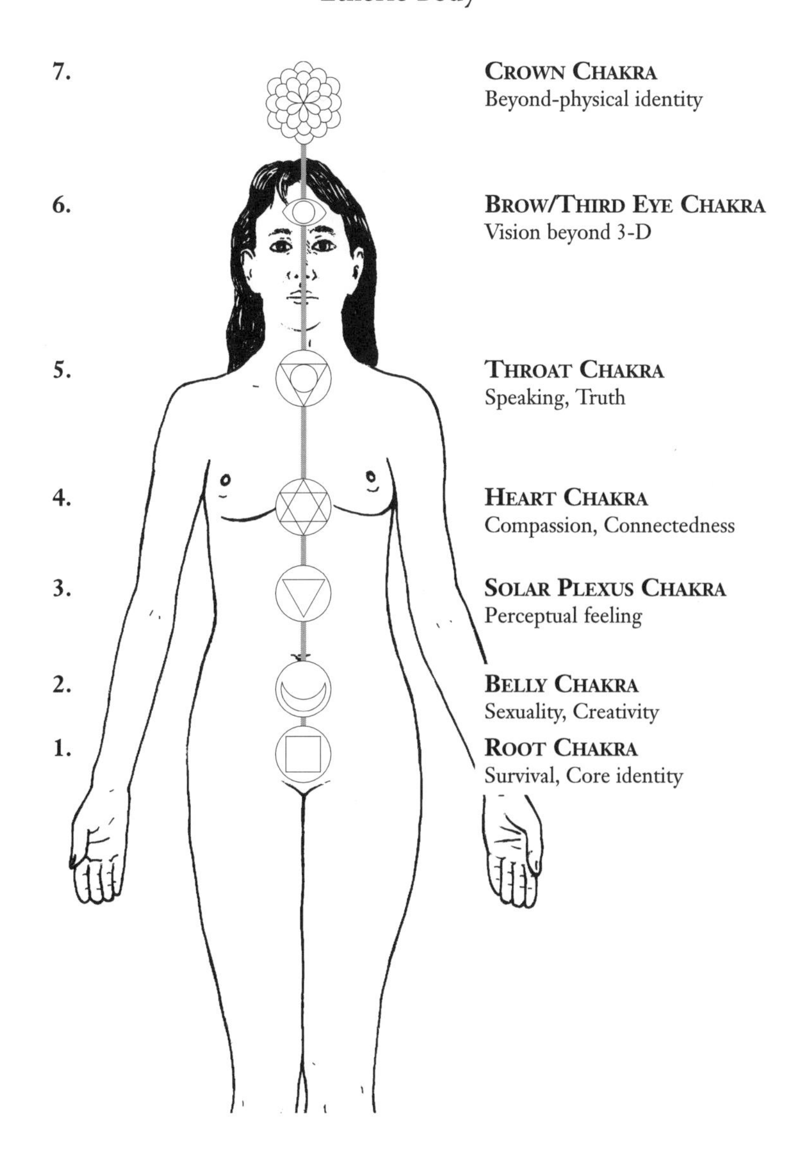

DIAGRAM 2. THE HARA LINE CHAKRAS
Emotional/Astral Body

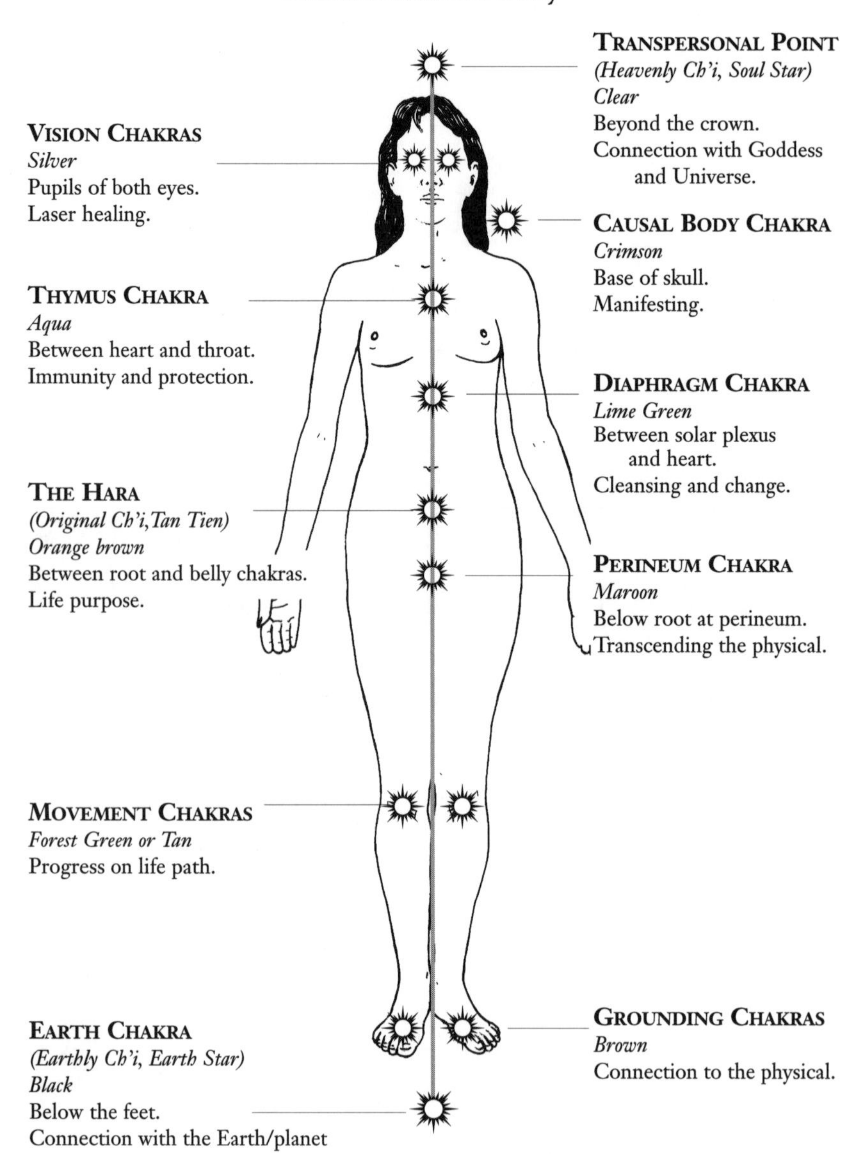

Mental Body

At the next level is the *Mental Body* with access to the mind grid, Earth grid, and universal grid. Buddhist philosophy states that all reality is created by the mind, and the mind grid is where one's concept of reality is developed and stored. The mind grid appears psychically as a golden screen of intersecting horizontal and vertical lines. Where thought forms or thought processes are outmoded or no longer working, the grid appears dim and tangled and knotted. Karma is stored in the mind grid—and healed there—as karmic beliefs and patterns are programmed into it. The best possible analogy to the mind grid is a computer.

The Earth grid is the collective thoughts, beliefs, and consciousness of the planet. The personal mind grid intersects with the Earth grid, and in some places looks very tangled indeed. Energy overload from the Earth changes has been known to temporarily damage the Earth grid, causing the energy screen to appear fallen like a pile of pick-up-sticks. Communication and clear thinking on the planet suffer until the grid is repaired, hopefully with a few outmoded thought forms removed. Clearing and healing individual karma and thought forms effect changes in the Earth grid, reflecting again that the Earth changes are happening from an individual level.

The galactic or universal grid is the "mind" grid of consciousnesses from other planets. While the Earth grid interfaces with the universal grid, conscious connection at this level is still slight for most people. It is increasing, however, as more other-planetary healers and helpers are joining to aid

Earth and Earth people during the changes. The mental body's connection to the next outer body level, spiritual body, is the Celestial Template, which also connects the crown and transpersonal point chakras in a much stepped-down form.

The Spiritual Body

The *Spiritual Body* contains several energy layers and is a cocoon that surrounds all the energy levels below it. The Higher Self resides at this energy level. When accessed she is the Maiden of the Goddess triad and may be brought into the closer-to-physical levels with some preparation. Once brought in, the Higher Self joins and merges with the Astral Twin and Etheric Double for escalated spiritual growth and conscious awareness. Her energy is intensely ecstatic to experience, as is the energy of all of the other "selves."

The Causal Body

The *Causal Body* is beyond the spiritual body level and is connected to it through the I-Am Template. It contains two layers, the Essence Self/Star Body level (lower level) and the core soul/Oversoul (higher level). Each of these energy layers offers access to a personality twin, the Essence Self/Star Self at the lower level and the Goddess Self/Oversoul at the higher. The Essence Self or Star Self is our central spiritual consciousness. She is who all our many incarnations evolve from, our central self. When brought into conscious energy she appears as an angel (the angels are our Essence and Goddess Selves!), and as the Mother of the Goddess Triad. When accessed, she will join and merge with the Higher Self (who

DIAGRAM 3. THE TEMPLATES AND ENERGY BODIES

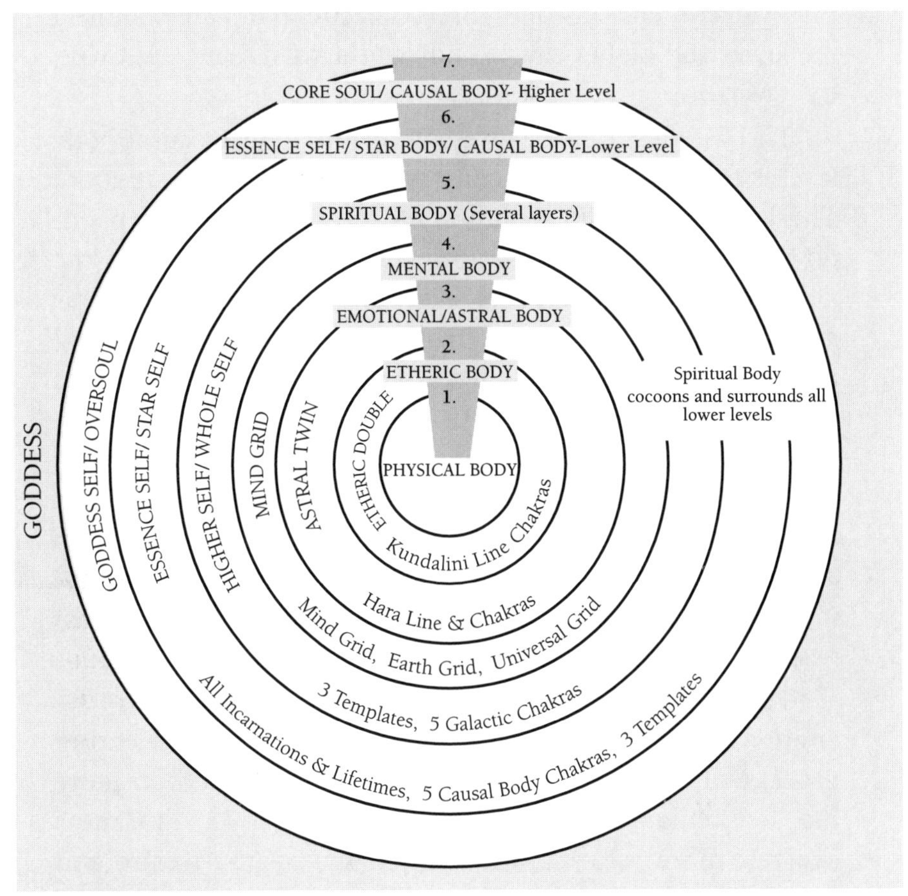

TEMPLATES:

1. KA: Connects Physical Body to Etheric Body, connects Root and Perineum chakras
2. ETHERIC: Connects Etheric Body to Emotional/Astral Body, connects Heart and Thymus
3. KETHERIC: Connects Emotional Body to Mental Body, connects Third Eye and Causal Body chakras
4. CELESTIAL: Connects Mental Body to Spiritual Body, connects Crown and Transpersonal Point chakras
5. I-AM: Connects Spiritual Body to Higher Self, Essence Self/Star Self, Core Soul and Oversoul/Goddess Self, connects via Galactic chakras (beyond the body entirely)
6. Three Galactic: Brings the Star Body/Essence Self into the Spiritual Body levels, connects Star Self to Higher Self
7. Three Causal Body: Brings the Goddess Self/Oversoul in, connects Oversoul to Essence Self, connection with Goddess.

is already merged with the Astral Twin and Etheric Double). Five galactic chakras and three Galactic Templates connect the lower and higher causal body levels, the Essence Self with the Oversoul.

The Goddess Self or Oversoul at the higher causal body level is the farthest known energy layer in Earth incarnation. This is who we are in our fullest life force energy, not stepped-down to accommodate the lowered energy vibrations of the body and nearer-to-physical levels. Five causal body chakras and three Causal Templates bring the Goddess Self/Oversoul in, connecting the Oversoul to the Essence Self. This is the Crone wisdom level of the Goddess triad, and she may be accessed and brought into consciousness. When this is done, the Goddess Self connects and merges with the Essence/Star Self, who is in turn merged with the Higher Self, Astral Twin and Etheric Double. When these energies are fully integrated into consciousness, however transformed so our consciousness can integrate them, we are truly Goddess.

Though described in terms of an ascending order, the energy bodies are a continuous and interconnecting process of beingness. They have been described as more like a circular pie than a vertical ladder. As awareness evolves, more information will emerge on the nature and function of these bodies. When all of the energy selves are merged and integrated, the Goddess herself is able to enter and fill our energy at all levels.

Animals also have these energy levels, as well as the personality energy "selves." My dogs, for example, already had their Etheric, Astral, Higher, and Essence Selves integrated, with only the Goddess Self to be brought in. While the other "selves" were definitely dogs (and dog angels!), the Goddess Self was clearly human in both animals. Pets also have a developed kundalini and hara line chakra system, but unlike humans, it is not in vertical alignment. Animals that work closely with people may perhaps be incarnated fragments of human souls. We have as much to learn about animal energy as we do about our own.

The connection between this complex structure of energy bodies to karmic healing and energy balancing will become more evident as this book unfolds.

Reincarnation

WESTERN CULTURE'S DENIAL OF REINCARNATION is the central source of its societal and moral decline. The denial removes accountability from human actions, as well as removes the empowerment of choice and the knowledge of having a place in the universal plan. It removes an awareness of order in the universe and for many people cancels their belief in a divine source. "Do unto others" has little meaning without the necessary addition, "what you send out returns." It also has little meaning without the knowledge that *you* will return. Where death is seen as the soul's final closure, avoidance of death becomes the ultimate goal, a goal often taken beyond the limits of compassion and common sense. Human choices, needs, and actions seem to have little to explain them if reincarnation is not taken into account.

Where there is no concept of the eternity of the soul there is little respect for life or for the Earth. People and animals are seen as expendable, and so are the planet's resources. Since death at the end of a very short lifetime seems the final ending, there is no need to conserve the rain forests, protect endangered species, find renewable alternatives for fossil fuels, or prevent the destruction of the ozone layer. If the resources last for one's own lifetime, it's enough. By contrast, Native Americans traditionally test their actions by taking into account their consequences to the seventh future generation. How many in the seventh generation will themselves be alive to see the results?

People without belief in reincarnation act on impulse, on what they feel they can get away with for now. If there are no immediate consequences, they feel they have prevailed. But what if the accounting comes in another lifetime? What if death is not the end, and what if the soul continues for eternity? What if the death of a damaged or used up body is a blessing providing a new and whole body? What if a person must eventually live with the depredations to the Earth (or the conservation of the Earth) she causes now? What if she must experience in turn her violence or dishonesty (or gentleness and integrity) to other people, or her mistreatment (or protection) of animals? What if everything one does to or for others, good or bad, returns to affect one's own life? And what if every unhealed trauma must finally and compassionately be healed? All of this is so.

Reincarnation was a central doctrine of early Judaism and Christianity, as well as intrinsic to Eastern religions, Islam, Buddhism, and Hinduism, and many African and Native American tribes. The concept was eliminated from Judaism and Catholicism by the fifth century. Judaism considered it too complex for the masses to understand, but the esoteric

Kabalists still accept it. Catholicism removed it from doctrine in 553 CE and declared it heretical in 1274 and 1439 in its attempt to make people more dependent upon Church political control and authority. They replaced it with a rewarding heaven for the docile faithful and a punishing hell for wrongdoers and independents—both distortions of Hindu and Buddhist concepts that Jesus would have known about. Yet, despite every attempt to suppress belief in reincarnation over several centuries, newspaper and Gallup polls of the 1980s stated that 29% of people polled in England and America believed in reincarnation and karma. With the influence of New Age material and many people's experience with past life literature and regression techniques, that figure has most surely increased today.

Wiccans have always believed in reincarnation and karma as a central facet of the Goddess religion. The life force is defined in Goddess cosmology as progressing in a never ending spiral of birth, life, death, and rebirth. Every ending is a new beginning, whether it be in the turning of the cycles of the year or the turning of the cycles of incarnation. After one dies, she returns to life again, just as the Earth blooms again after winter's barrenness. Birth is a progression from infancy to maturity to eventual death, and death is the transition to a time of rest followed by another rebirth and the start of a new cycle. As we are all sparks of the life force of the Goddess, what happens on the planet also happens to each individual who lives upon it. We die and are reborn many times.

The concept offers the comfort and certainty of a universal plan. The short human life span does not allow for full understanding of what it means to be human, full learning about the oneness of all life, so repeated incarnations afford the opportunity to complete the lessons. Life's purpose is to learn what it means to be in a body, what it means to be human in every aspect of life, both positive and negative. We are expected to experience all things, to learn living from all angles, until we have done it all. As people in incarnation mature with age and experience, so do souls mature and grow with the variety and lessons of multiple lifetimes.

Karma is the mechanism that connects all of a person's lifetimes and sets the course of study for each soul. Everyone must experience life at least once as a mother, father, and child. Everyone must have prosperous lifetimes and poor lifetimes, healthy lifetimes and those plagued by illness or deformity, empowered and disempowered lifetimes, lives filled with love and lives devoid of it. Everyone has been incarnated in all of the races and all parts of the world. To learn interdependence, everyone has her soul mate, her partner through all or most of her lifetimes. Both partners will experience being male and female, and they will have heterosexual, lesbian, and gay partnerships with their mates. Every soul must experience all things—and the opposites of all things. It is required at least once to live a negative or criminal lifetime to teach us how that feels. We have also all been treated badly to teach us compassion for others.

We are expected to learn honesty, compassion, love of oneself and others, respect for animals and the Earth. Each incarnation requires service to people or to the planet, and as souls evolve that service deepens to become the purpose of each incarnation. Evolution of the soul is the curriculum, and living is the university. Each lifetime is another course of study. When the schooling is complete, souls are offered a choice of returning to help others or remaining in the between-life state as a guide to those in bodies. Those who return are called bodhisattvas and many are incarnated on Earth now. To reach that completion, all karma must be cleared and healed, all learning in all opposites experienced, and the soul must evolve to a recognition that all life is one. Realization of what has been accomplished and what remains to be accomplished is a central factor in reincarnation and in the conditions of each rebirth.

How do we know all this? Young children often retain memories of their most recent past lives and talk about them unless stopped by adults. Many adults experience dreams or déjà vu, flashbacks of former times, often triggered by a visit to the place where the previous lifetime occurred. They may be curiously attracted to a place or an era and seem intuitively to know in detail the culture they have never studied or visited before. A person may be strongly attracted to, repelled by, or even afraid of someone they have just met without any rational this-life explanation. Lovers often strongly feel that they have been together before. Phobias may be present in one's life that have no logical reason for occurring. These phobias may turn out to be quite logical when past life traumas are uncovered. People who learn to meditate or who develop psychically in other ways may experience spontaneous images of past life friends, enemies, and situations.

Hypnosis has opened the field of controlled past life exploration, from the first popularly documented case in 1954 when Morey Bernstein regressed Virginia Tigue into a past life as Bridey Murphy in Ireland in the 1800s. Much controversy followed Bernstein's subsequent book, along with the discovery by hypnotists and therapists that past life regression could cure a variety of phobias and ills. By simply viewing in hypnotic regression the past life source of a difficulty, the problem was often released. Cures of psychological aberrations, dis-eases, phobias, and relationship problems were reported. While many traditional therapists avoid regression into past lives, many others make positive use of it, and many more were forced into belief simply by repeated proofs. These discoveries were the beginnings of karmic healing.

In the last few decades, hypnosis and meditation have made thorough inquiry into the nature of past lives, the between-life state, reincarnation, and karma. More availability of Buddhist and Hindu writings in translation has sparked people's curiosity to know more and to discover the truth for themselves. Books are now being written by people who have gone through near-death experiences and have had their lives changed by them. People want to know who they are in terms of who they have been before. When they attempt past life regression, few are disappointed. The knowledge is transformative—once you know you have been here before, been here many times, life and death take on new meaning and much that has been unexplained becomes evident.

Learning our past is a simple process. Many books describe self-hypnosis and meditative techniques to regress to a past lifetime, but there is a simpler way. The process begins with a basic meditative state. Find a quiet half hour when you will not be interrupted, and take the phone off the hook. In a darkened or candlelit room, sit comfortably on the floor or on a straight-backed chair. The lotus meditation position is unnecessary; arms and legs should be uncrossed and the body made comfortable but not so relaxed as to fall asleep. You may wish to cast a protective circle, or simply ask that energies of only the highest good be allowed to participate in your inquiries. Take several slow, deep breaths and calm your body and your thoughts.

When you feel still, ask to speak with the Lords (or call them Angels) of Karma. You will perceive a presence in some subtle way, visually or by sensation or sound. Treat these Beings with great respect, they are the directors of our karma and of our many incarnations. Ask to be shown a past life that has relevance to this lifetime, perhaps relevance to a difficulty you are experiencing now. Sit quietly with a cleared, still mind to receive the impressions that will come. You may see pictures or perceive information by hearing, bodily sensation, or in other ways. You may or may not understand what you are being shown; ask for clarification if you wish. If what you are shown seems traumatic, you may ask to "watch it like a movie" without feeling distress or pain. If what you see seems negative, you may ask the Lords of Karma to heal the situation or the lifetime, and to heal its influence on your lifetime now.

When you have seen what you need, thank the Lords of Karma and return to now. You may ask to see more than one lifetime in a meditative sitting, but at first it is best to ask for just one. You will have a lot to think about later, even with one incarnation, especially if you have not been aware of your past lives before. After the meditation you may receive further impressions of the lifetime you were shown—flashbacks, dreams, or "just knowing." The Lords of Karma will usually pick for you a past life that needs healing, and reviewing it and asking them to heal it will be important for your current situation. You may repeat the meditation daily to learn more about your incarnational past, your soul's Akashic Record. In each case, where a situation has been negative or traumatic, ask to heal it. Your understanding of who you are as a soul on a spiritual journey will grow considerably.

After reviewing a number of past lives, their pattern will come into focus. You may be aware, for example, that you have had a number of past lives with your current mate and that most of them have had relationship difficulties similar to those you are having now. You may be poor or oppressed in this lifetime and learn that you have often been poor or oppressed in your past lives. When you are aware of a pattern, you may do something to heal it. Do the meditation described above, this time asking the Lords of Karma to show you the lifetime where the pattern you perceive began. You may be shown a lifetime you have not seen before, or possibly a new facet of one you have already witnessed. When you understand how the source situation has created the pattern you perceive, you may ask the Lords of Karma to heal both the lifetime that is the source and the pattern. You will have some perception of whether or not this may be done at this time. Thank them, and come back to now.

Use of this process in depth for full karmic healing and release follows in later chapters. For now, what is important is to learn that you have had many past lives and to learn what some of them were like. You may also wish to learn about birth and death, and what existence is like between lifetimes. One exercise might be to ask the Lords of Karma to show you a *peaceful* death in one of your past lives. You will be surprised at how wondrous and free of trauma the death process is. Experiencing your birth, even a normal one, is far more painful and traumatic. If you choose to do this, ask to "watch it like a movie" without distress or pain. In other meditations, you may also ask to be taken to the between-life state. By the end of these explorations you will no longer fear death or reincarnation.

What about asking to view future lifetimes? For the most part this is tricky, and it is usually discouraged. The past and present determine the course of the future. What you have already learned does not need to be repeated, and you are still learning in this life. Each day's growth in this lifetime changes your future incarnations, and what you see today can change by tomorrow and will certainly change by the end of this incarnation. If you are still interested in future life progression, do the above meditation, but first ask the Lords of Karma if it is appropriate for you to be shown a future life. If they indicate that it is not, drop it. Never argue with them. If they show you a future life, it may be a lesson of what needs to be learned now to prevent a later difficulty. Take the lesson seriously and do the work required.

Animals also have evolving souls and karma to be healed. If you have a dog or cat you feel close to, you may ask to see one of their past lives. Place your hands gently on the quiet or sleeping pet, and ask to speak with the Lords of Karma. Ask to be shown a past life of the animal that has relevance for this lifetime. You may be surprised to discover that your current pet was with you in another body in the past, in this or other incarnations. The animal may also have experienced traumatic lives that need healing. When you see the situation, your pet will likely indicate that she sees it, too, by becoming restless or sometimes whining. Ask the Lords of Karma to heal any abused or traumatic past experiences for the animal, in the life where it happened and as it affects her lifetime now.

Past life regression is the beginning of working with and healing your karma. Karma may be defined as the accrued lessons of past lifetimes, particularly those remaining lessons that you have agreed to complete and release in the present incarnation. The beginning of healing karma is to become familiar with the idea of reincarnation and your own past lives and to make your acquaintance with the Lords of Karma. More discussion on what the lessons may be, how they operate, and how to heal them follows, and much more work with the Lords (or Angels) of karma who direct our lifetimes' learnings.

The Four Kinds of Karma

DIFFICULTIES FROM PAST LIVES THAT SURFACE to affect this lifetime fall into four primary categories. The categories are designed to work from the viewpoint of this lifetime, tracing current problems back to their sources that may be from the past. If you have knowledge of some of your past lives, you will become aware of patterns, difficulties, or situations that repeat from lifetime to lifetime and continue in the present. These also seem to fall into the four categories. A simple but powerful beginning for clearing them from the viewpoint of the past was given in the last chapter. The full process of healing and releasing karmic patterns and situations is given in detail later. The purpose of this section and the next is to offer a more detailed understanding of karma and how it repeats from lifetime to lifetime.

Understanding karma from the four categories is a way of making very evident the effect of past lives on the present. Our many lifetimes are interconnected, and the lessons of them are intertwined. A lifetime is not over when one dies. Its major and often minor events carry forward as part of one's energy makeup to affect every future incarnation. In this present lifetime, previous experiences and events affect our outlook and personalities. It is the same with events from past lives. We do not stop at death; one lifetime's experiences create the situations and learnings of the next, though incarnations repeating a situation or trauma may not be consecutive. When something in one's Akashic Record of lifetimes has not worked, has been traumatic, has caused harm or been negative to oneself or others, the situation will repeat until it is faced and healed.

The agent for healing a karmic pattern is always realization. When you understand what has not worked, what has been wrong, and where the mistake is, it becomes relatively easy to make a new choice and change the pattern. Karma is always based upon free will and choice. If something isn't working, try a different and more positive way of dealing with it. Much karmic release today also involves realizing what is wrong in a relationship or situation and healing past karma so the future can incorporate the changed choices. Where in older times karma was considered to be an irreparable, irrevocable fate or destiny, it is not so today. Almost anything can be healed, but the realization must be there first. You must know that something is wrong in your life, why it is wrong for you, and have a wish to change the pattern for the better.

Despite the subtle psychology of traditional religions, guilt, blame, and shame are of no benefit in this process. Everyone has done negative things at some time or another, everyone has committed crimes, and everyone has had unpleasant lifetimes. Everyone has suffered, and suffering is a major mechanism for soul growth, maturity, and evolution. The purpose of being shown such negativity and suffering from the past is not to make one feel guilty, but to effect change in attitude and awareness. The purpose is to create a realization of "that was wrong, I won't do it again," and to gain compassion for oneself and others. Blame is also irrelevant and like guilt it obstructs rather than furthers the karmic release process. Self-blame is as destructive as blaming others.

Everyone has had lifetimes where they have been victimized, and they have victimized other people. The purpose of becoming conscious of these situations is to create change so the lesson does not have to be repeated or returned to in some way, so the suffering does not continue. Once you have seen the error and changed the attitude and behaviors, the learning is complete and the karma can then be cleared. The person who harmed you in a past life whom you know today is very different now from who they were in the past. Neither you nor they merit blame.

Shame is also a negative reaction to past life issues. Where guilt is about something you have done and blame puts the guilt upon others, shame is about who you intrinsically are. Since we are all Goddess and made by Goddess, we have nothing to be ashamed of, though we do have to take responsibility. We are each part of the life force of divinity, of the

Earth, the universe and all that lives, and we can justifiably take pride in that gift. Negative self-image is the trait that most needs healing in women today, and inflated self-image in men. We are all part of the ultimate magick and wonder of life on this planet. There is no room for shame and no need of it.

The four karmic categories are simple and evident. They are *dis-eases, relationships, life situations, and character traits or negative habits*. It is fairly easy to look at one's current life and find a number of items in each category that need work. The trick of karmic release is not only to identify the problems in this life, but to identify the patterns of their recurrence in past lives and their sources in the lifetimes where the patterns began. Since we have had innumerable past lives on Earth—some researchers say thousands—and countless more on other planets, the task of locating the source of anything may seem next to impossible.

This is not so. The Lords of Karma are willing in this lifetime for us to clear all or most of our Earth karma. The karma from other planets is rarely relevant for our Earth Akashic Records and will not often be involved. When we ask to understand or heal the source of a difficulty in this lifetime, the lifetime we need to see will be revealed. This granting of karmic dispensation in this lifetime has made the process very easy. The Be-ings that order our karma on Earth are now ready for us to heal it and willing to help us in every way with the methods and techniques for doing so. Karmic grace is a part of the Earth changes and the healing of the planet.

Dis-eases

The first category or kind of karma includes physical or nonphysical dis-eases or conditions. This is probably what people think of immediately when they want dispensation from a negative situation in this life. It's actually the last thing to approach the Lords of Karma with, as all the emotional and mental sources of the dis-ease must be first cleared before they will grant a release. Every dis-ease has its emotional and/or mental component or cause. Some dis-eases cannot be healed—the damage to the body is too great, but if nothing else is granted the dis-ease will not be repeated in coming lives. The person experiencing the dis-ease can also be made more comfortable or given partial healing, if full healing cannot be attained.

Dis-eases in this category include more than those of the body. I have worked with people at healing their mental and emotional conditions and achieved positive changes. The results have shown me that absolutely nothing in human life is hopeless. In physical dis-eases, the mid-range of ills seems easiest to clear. Avoid asking to heal a cold, flu, or skin scrape, as such conditions are self-limiting and require no angelic assistance. On the other hand, a person who has been born with a physical deformity may not be able to change it. I have seen optimistic results with such things as muscular dystrophy, spinal curvature, attention deficit disorder, multiple personality disorder, chronic insomnia, inability to quiet the mind, tumors, lifelong allergies, injuries, sores and bone breaks that refuse to heal, spirit possession, fibromyalgia, chronic fatigue, and chronic back pain. Remember that these were not medical healings, but if karmic release is granted, conditions may change for the better.

Relationships

The next category of karma and karmic healing is relationships. Our mates in this lifetime have been with us in many other incarnations, and we have built patterns of behavior with them that may not all be positive. Every life has its confusions, difficult situations, and left-over pain to clear. The problem in a particular lifetime may not be with the relationship itself but with the traumas of an earlier life or death. Circumstances like a traumatic death or separation in a past incarnation can prevent soul mates from accepting each other in this life. One or both may unconsciously fear a repetition of the trauma. Difficulties in today's marriage or relationship may also come from the slights, poor judgments, infidelities, or misunderstandings of past lives. Those who are true soul mates have been together through many lifetimes with countless opportunities for both love and difficulty. Now is the time to clear and heal the past for the peace and benefit of the present and future.

Relationships with others who are *not* soul mates also require healing. These include one's children, parents, business partners, coworkers, teachers, friends, other relatives, and people who have done us wrong or harm. Parents and children can provide our greatest karmic lessons and challenges, as can people who have hurt us. As we incarnate in groups and in interchanging roles, our parents from this lifetime may have been our children, teachers, friends, or enemies in other incarnations. Someone who has hurt us in this life may have hurt us before. As with our soul mates, there is usually a long karmic background with anyone who is close to us or important to us now positively or negatively. Viewing the source of friction between any two people can offer great understanding of why the friction exists. Often simply knowing the past life source is enough to clear it and prevent its continuing.

I have found it important to ask for "complete karmic healing" with any close relationship, whether there is friction or not. By doing so, all the problems are released, though all may have not yet been revealed, and the relationship will run far more smoothly. It is very useful to do this especially with one's mate, parents, children, and business associates. An ounce of prevention, in even a harmonious relationship, can give a pound of cure. Where there is conflict between two people or even with a group, understanding the source can be instructive in healing it.

It is necessary to note, however, that when asking for karmic healing involving another person, the healing can be given only to *you*. The other person must ask for it directly if she wants it. When you ask to heal a relationship you are asking to heal *your* part in it—and that usually is enough. It is a grave error to try to change someone else's karma without their consent and participation, a breach of ethics that is not permitted, and may in itself carry negative karmic consequences.

Life Situations

The third category of karma and karmic change is life situations. If, for example, you have worked hard all of your life but are still struggling in poverty, the reason may be karmic. By finding the past life where the poverty began, you may gain an understanding of what you need to learn from it, and having learned it can then release and change it. You may find that you are poor because you abused your wealth in a prior incarnation. You may find you are poor because some guilt in this life or in a past incarnation convinced you that you deserved to be poor. People who have been nuns or monks in the past and taken vows of poverty may need to discover and release those vows.

Often a decision that was positive in a past life setting carries over to the present, where it is no longer positive. This can happen also in our present lives, as a decision made by a child that is positive at the time may no longer be useful and may even be harmful to her as an adult. A child's choice to repress the memory of a trauma she cannot deal with can mean emotional survival for the child but wreak havoc on her psyche and development when she is grown. The adult can handle the memory and heal it, but must have some idea of its presence to begin with. It's the same with past life traumas, and in the case of negative life situations this is often the mechanism to discover and clear. If your negative situation began in this lifetime, asking to see the source will also reveal that information and karmic healing will release it.

Negative Character Traits and Habits

The fourth category to clear through karmic release is negative personality or character traits and bad habits. I have used this process to help women quit smoking, and though they still had to do the work of quitting and go through the detoxification of their bodies, the process was far easier and faster than it otherwise would have been. Phobias come under this category, also. Most of these are direct past life carryovers, and understanding the source often immediately releases them. The woman who fears water was probably drowned in one or more past lifetimes. Someone who fears heights may have fallen to her death from a high place or have been greatly injured. Anorexia may have resulted from having starved to death in the past; the source of anorexia in several women was death by starvation in a concentration camp.

Recurrent dreams are often karmic, also. They may show fragments of a past life situation in an attempt to bring it to conscious attention for healing. Often the dream makes no sense until you ask the Lords of Karma for its source and release. In one case, a woman's dream involved being under the Earth, alone and afraid. In its past life source, she had been a miner left to explore a cavern alone. Her partner had gone and the rope access ladder fell; she was trapped in the cave and eventually died there. The partner who left her is now her lover. By opening the memory, the dream that has haunted her for years stopped, and her relationship greatly improved.

A negative character trait people have found difficult to clear can also be released by working with it karmically. In my own case, I asked for help in talking over other people; I had to learn to let them finish speaking before I answered. I had tried unsuccessfully to break this habit for years, but one request for karmic release stopped it permanently. Other examples are mannerisms like continually pulling on a lock of one's hair or biting one's fingernails. Most of us have such habits.

A friend had great difficulty in keeping her house neat. Her refrigerator was always filled with spoiled leftovers, which she would never eat, and she hated and avoided grocery shopping and cooking. She and her children ate at fast-food restaurants, though she knew better. When she asked for help, we went to the Lords of Karma. The common thread seemed to be food, and we asked for the source of her food issues. She was shown several past lives where she had either been a house servant permitted to eat nothing but leftovers, or she had been responsible for cooking meal after meal for large numbers of people. She had been an army cook and also a cook for workers of a large farm. She had cleaned others' houses in many lifetimes with little thanks. Once she saw and released the past lives and the damage from them, her housekeeping resistance lessened considerably. We were told that it would gradually disappear.

The four categories—dis-eases, relationships, life situations, and character traits or bad habits—offer a framework for understanding and working to clear most areas of negative karma. The meditation in the previous chapter is a place to start. The full process will come a little later in this book. It is important at this time to understand the functioning and mechanisms of karma before attempting to change it for oneself.

The Process of Rebirth

HOW KARMA IS CARRIED FROM LIFETIME TO lifetime, and how karmic decisions are made for each lifetime is vital knowledge for working to heal karmic problems. We are much more than our physical bodies. Most of our selves and lives, in fact, operate outside of our physical levels. We are unaware of this for two reasons. At the time of birth the "karmic veil" is drawn and we forget our out-of-body life and past lives. There is reason for this; we must learn to focus our full attention on the learning of the current lifetime, without comparisons and distractions. Somehow this seems terribly unfair, considering our difficulty in regaining even a small amount of past life and soul knowledge. Little or none of this tantalizing information is available to us during most of our Earth incarnations.

The other reason is the influence, at least in the West, of the dominant religious authorities. Catholicism and Protestantism were state religions in centuries past, concerned more with authority and control of people than with spirituality. The masses were kept more docile by having to go to priests for every aspect of religion, and the priesthood was ruled by both Church and government. When doctrine held that salvation must be gained or lost in one lifetime, as people without knowledge of reincarnation were told, dependence and fear were fostered in the people. Everyone except the male nobility and some clergy was kept uneducated, to reinforce that dependence upon Church and state. Punishment for independent thinking could also be severe—the Crusades and Inquisition ensured strict doctrine with death as the only alternative. Some outstanding women like Teresa of Avila and Hildegard of Bingen walked the fine line between sainthood and execution, but many more did not survive.

Jews in Europe were kept totally subjugated. Jewish doctrine like the Christian declared questions of spirituality to be beyond the understanding of the masses. Though many Jewish males were more educated than their gentile counterparts, women were not educated at all. Deep thinking on subjects like death, karma, and reincarnation was left to the esoteric Kabalists, and few people were versed in their teachings.

Nine million freethinking witches were burned during the Inquisition. Any knowledge they may have had about death and rebirth was lost, along with the state of the art healing techniques that they knew. Evidence of psychic ability was grounds for burning at the stake in the Inquisition, too, and this knowledge has also been submerged until recently. It is ironic that in the name of religion we have lost any knowledge of who we are. This ultimate censorship was and is a clear failure of the most sacred trust. Hopefully that is changing and the knowledge returning in this New Age.

The information being regained today on death, rebirth, reincarnation, and karma come primarily from two sources. In the 1920s Helena Blavatsky and the Theosophical Society she started were interested in Buddhism and Hinduism. Still active, Theosophy opened the West to the rich spirituality of India and Tibet. Translations and discussion of especially Buddhist texts and philosophy have appeared in the past 70 years, emerging from the interest Theosophy began. Compelling teachers like the Dalai Lama and various gurus who have come to the West have inspired many people to learn more.

The other source for information on rebirth comes from hypnotic regression, past life regression, accounts of near death experiences, and the psychic meditation work of many people. An increasing body of literature is developing that describes the process of death and rebirth and the between-life state. When so many different inquirers receive knowledge that complements each other's studies, a body of viable information begins to develop. That growing information and my own psychic explorations are the basis of the material that follows. A further source is Dr. Michael Newton's book *Journey of Souls*, which transcribes the sessions of a number of individuals under hypnosis on these subjects.

When a person dies, the nonphysical aspects of Be-ing separate from the physical. The body remains to be buried or cremated, but the nonphysical "selves" return to the soul worlds from whence they came at the person's birth. This is what is meant by the severing of the Silver Cord, the separation of the unseen energy levels from the physical body at death. The chakras at hara and kundalini lines stop transmitting energy. The etheric body dies with the physical and is discarded—its purpose of bringing the life force into the physical Be-ing is no longer needed. The Etheric Double does not die, but moves upward to merge with the Astral Twin on the emotional body level.

The emotional body retreats upward, and its energy is absorbed into that of the mental body and mind grid. Emotional damage is carried into the mental body as an energy pattern and held there, to reincarnate when the soul chooses a new lifetime. Negative mental patterns and thought forms are also held at this level in a method similar to computer coding. Unhealed emotional and mental body damage is retained in the vibration of the mental body, and is repeated in the makeup of the new incarnation. It is not healed in the between-life state, as damage originating in incarnation can be healed only while the soul is incarnated in a body. This is where karma originates. The Astral Twin moves through the emotional and mental levels and is absorbed into the Higher Self at the spiritual body; the infant and child "selves" grow into the maturity of the Maiden.

The spiritual body, holding the coded information and vibration of the emotional and mental levels and "selves," then ascends to the level of the Essence Self and is absorbed by it. The Higher Self joins the Essence Self as the bodies merge; the Maiden becomes the Mother. The Essence Self, at the lower level of the causal body, is the aggregate of all the soul's many incarnations, and all the learning of all the incarnations is held there. This is the angelic level. All individuals' Essence and Goddess Selves are angels. Angels are not a Christian concept, nor simply another name for spirit guides (which reach us from the spiritual body level). We are all angels.

The Akashic Record, the soul record of all an individual's many lifetimes, is kept at the lower causal body level. Perhaps this soul level *is* the Akashic Record itself. It is the Essence Self, the Mother aspect, that determines what life lessons have been learned from the past incarnation, and what learning still needs to be done in coming lifetimes. The person does not present herself for judgment, but for assessment and evaluation. All the bodies and selves to this point have merged with the lower causal body and Essence Self, but the Essence Self remains autonomous and does not merge further upward. The Lords of Karma work from the level of our Essence Self and Akashic Record, but enter our in-body consciousness at the mental body.

The core soul or Oversoul, at the higher causal body level, is an aggregate of Essence Selves and is actually a group soul or group of souls. The core soul is the Goddess Self, the Goddess' Crone aspect of eternal wisdom. The Oversoul or Goddess Self does not enter incarnation; it is the Essence Self that divides into many lifetimes. Each Essence Self returning from an incarnation brings information and learning about life in the body back to the core soul. Twenty-five to thirty Essence Selves participate in one Goddess Self/core soul, who has the role of teacher or overseer of the Essence Selves in her care. When each Essence Self has completed her full spiritual evolution and all required incarnations, she separates from the group and becomes a new Goddess Self with other Essence Selves to lead and care for.

The process of moving upward to the Essence and Goddess Selves is made in the between-life state. It does not happen immediately after death, but in a progression of preparatory stages. The length of time spent at each stage is individual, depending upon assimilation of the soul's learning about her last lifetime at each level and her desire to progress onward. Time spent in the between-life state has been compared to study at a university. The just ended lifetime is analyzed and evaluated; it is compared with other past lives, and decisions are made as to what experiences have been finished and which ones still need to be lived. A soul does not need to progress to the Essence Self level to be able to reincarnate again, but only to the spiritual body level. From that point she may go forward to the Essence Self and Goddess/Oversoul or return to incarnate in a new physical body. A soul may progress to the Essence Self development level and still reincarnate, usually as a highly evolved Be-ing in service to the planet. Once she progresses to the Goddess Self/ Oversoul/core soul level, she will not reincarnate in a body.

The decision to reincarnate is made by the Essence Self, who then starts a part of her Be-ing back through the process.

Up to six incarnations from one Essence Self can be in bodies at once, though they will seldom meet. Soul mates who have completed their learning with each other and still wish to remain together may incarnate as a single strand from the Essence Self, which is then divided into two incarnations. Once a couple is allowed to join permanently and eternally, the two souls merge into one. They are "sealed into the light" and may then incarnate together in one body, with two separate consciousnesses. This is a blessing, a completion, and a great gift, as all souls were originally formed in joined pairs.

As the lower causal body contains the Akashic Record, it is the Essence Self that decides what primary lessons and experiences the soul must undergo in her next incarnation. With the basic decisions made, the soul descends to the spiritual body level, where the Higher Self separates and individuates from the Essence Self. The Higher Self of the new incarnation then works with the Lords of Karma to map out the conditions and situations of the coming lifetime. This may include choosing parents that will give the soul a start on accomplishing the decided lessons, and teachers that will influence her life's purpose and set her on her spiritual path. What that path will be, who her mate will be and the circumstances of their relationship, where she will live, and what race and gender she will take for the incarnation are also decided at this point. The soul's service to humanity and the planet is chosen, if not already established by the Essence Self, and the best way to accomplish that service is determined.

Challenges like handicaps and difficult circumstances are arranged, each with a specific purpose or a portion of that lifetime's lesson. The traumas, sufferings, hurts, negative thought forms, unfinished relationship issues, and soul damage retained from past lifetimes are taken into account, as well as other unresolved issues from other lifetimes recorded in the soul's Akashic Record. Some of these must be healed in the coming lifetime, while other unresolved issues are left for future incarnations. Those that must be met in the coming life are retained when the mental and emotional bodies separate from the spiritual body level to become operative in the new incarnation. Those that are not to appear in the new life are moved into the Akashic Record for future use.

All the choices and decisions of a coming lifetime are made with the consent of the soul who is to experience them. Decisions are made carefully with every possible aid from spirit guides, one's Higher Self, Essence Self, the Goddess, and the Lords of Karma. While it seems inexplicable that people would actually choose the sufferings they will experience, remember that they are chosen on a soul level where suffering means only that spiritual growth occurs and lessons are accomplished. At these levels there is no pain, and just as people forget the soul worlds when they are born, souls forget what pain means in the body once the bodies die. We agree to our lifetime learnings, but do not always choose how those learnings are to manifest. They are decisions made on nonconscious levels, for the greater good or necessary evolution.

By this time the soul has chosen her new body and is ready to enter it when the fetus is ready to be born. She may visit it in her Astral body once that "self" separates from the Higher Self and the new emotional level develops. The soul may move in and out as the fetus develops in the womb, but does not fully enter it until birth. It descends only as far as the Astral Twin before the birth, as the etheric body and Etheric Double are not released or activated until the fetus' live delivery.

In the soul's progress to a new lifetime, the Higher Self descends from the spiritual body levels into the newly reorganizing mental body. The mind grid forms the mental body of the new incarnation, transmits the decided-upon karma, and then generates the separation of the emotional body. The Astral Twin separates from the Higher Self to reside at the new emotional/astral level. The Etheric Double individuates from the Astral Twin at birth, and it in turn then activates the etheric body and etheric/kundalini chakras. The Etheric Double's connection to the body, and the activation of the etheric body, is made through the vagus nerve which becomes the autonomic nervous system of the physical body.

The hara line chakras are also activated at birth with the etheric chakras. This is done by the Etheric Double's separation from the Astral Twin and the subsequent separation of the energy lines. The Etheric Double remains permanently next to the physical body from here on, while the Astral Twin moves in and out of the body freely during infancy and throughout the life. Both Etheric and Astral "selves" are connected at the back of the heart chakra, with the other personality "selves" in line beyond them. This connection of "selves" and bodies is the Silver Cord.

Thus is life ended and returned to incarnation, and the Wheel of Life and Karma begins again.

The Lords of Karma

WHO ARE THE LORDS OF KARMA AND WHY DO they help us to clear our karmic debts and patterns at this time? Very little seems to have been written on these Be-ings, but we do know they are mentioned in both Indian writings and Old Testament Judaism. In Judaism they are called the Lipika, the Recording Angels of the Book of Life. The original Old Testament focus on judgment is karmic judgment, and this is probably also true of the New Testament and Revelations. Jesus came out of a Hebrew esoteric tradition, the Essenes, which may have had close ties to early Mahayana Buddhism. He may also have received training in Egypt, India, and Tibet. Christianity originally held the concept of karma and reincarnation and early Christians would have been aware of the Lords of Karma.

In Buddhism and Hinduism, karma is the direct manifestation of punishment and reward earned through a person's deeds or attachments (emotions). As accumulated in one lifetime, these deeds and attachments are returned to the soul in the next incarnation: For good or for bad "what you sow is what you reap." This version of the law of karma is implacable. What you do returns to you, often harshly, and life inevitably means suffering. The Lords of Karma confer the judgment and the punishment and there is no appeal. The only salvation for the individual in these philosophies is to complete the lessons and prevent further karma, positive or negative. It is karma still to be completed that makes reincarnation necessary, with ending the Wheel of Rebirth the ultimate goal.

Devout Hindus decline to do healing to help someone, for fear that doing so will give them karmic attachment (however positive) with that person. They also feel that by healing someone they have interfered with that person's karma, which makes it necessary for them to repeat the suffering in another incarnation to complete it. They will not help a starving or dying person lying on the streets of Calcutta, because they believe they would be interfering with the person's required fate. My own understanding of healing and karma is that if someone is to be helped, the healer is just a neutral channel for the will of Goddess.

Buddhism is gentler and more compassionate, though like Hinduism its intent is ending the Wheel of Rebirth. In the Buddhist concept, understanding how the world works, and how the mind (mental body, mind grid) creates karma and all reality, frees a person from its illusion, and from having to continue on the Wheel. That understanding is called enlightenment, the ultimate goal. In early Theravada

Buddhism, a person who attained enlightenment went to Parinirvana, into the nothingness of the Void, and never returned to Earth or incarnation again. Later Mahayana Buddhism offered the concept of the bodhisattva: those who have attained enlightenment may choose to return to help others achieve freedom. No one leaves Earth permanently until everyone leaves. Jesus was probably versed in Mahayana Buddhism, by the evidence of his teachings, and he was certainly a bodhisattva. The techniques in this book, while not Buddhist, can further each individual on the path to resolving karma for everyone.

Judaism offers the most familiar example of the workings of the Lords of Karma. For Jews, the Fall Equinox New Year celebration of Rosh Hashanah means the opening of the Akashic Record or each soul's Book of Life. For ten days the book is open, while God and the Recording Angels observe people's lives and determine their destinies for the coming year. In those ten days, one's karma for the year is written but can still be revised. On Yom Kippur, ten days after the New Year, the book and one's fate are sealed and become irrevocable. Most of the discussion of law and judgment in Judaism is karmic judgment and can be quite harsh.

When I first met the Lords of Karma, they seemed as implacable (and downright scary) as their reputation. I was introduced to them during a healing I received about five years ago. There was an issue in my life I needed help with, as no technique I'd used had made a difference. The healer directed me to ask for the presence of the Lords of Karma, and then to ask them what my karmic contract for that issue was. When I did so, a row of tall Be-ings covered in black robes came into my psychic vision. They did not speak and seemed quite displeased that I had asked for them to come. I asked about the contract and was given the information I requested, briefly and tersely.

The healer directed me to ask if the contract could be changed to allow for healing. When I did, the Lords of Karma wished to know what I would change the contract to. The healer warned me to be very careful wording my request, because, if it were granted, it would become irrevocable. She, I, my spirit guides, and the Astral Self of the other person in the contract discussed what to ask for and the exact wording of the request. When that was decided, I asked again for the Karmic Be-ings' presence and stated my request. I heard the single word "granted," and they were gone.

I was told by the healer that going to these Be-ings should be done only once in a lifetime, for a life or death reason, and only if all other possible options have failed. "Don't get them mad," she warned me. "You were born into a culture with relative freedom, hot water, and flush toilets. You don't want to starve in Somalia next time." By now I was thoroughly awed, but my request had been granted and the multicolored fireworks and rainbows I watched psychically for many nights after confirmed the changes. My healing work since that time has focused upon bringing the healing into the earthplane level, and it has now manifested through all the other bodies. Most karmic release work happens far more immediately once granted.

After this first meeting I was wary about returning to the Lords of Karma, but did so occasionally when doing healing for others. If someone came to me with a life-threatening, or life's peace-threatening issue that seemed otherwise unresolvable, I took them for karmic release. Some spectacular healings occurred, but because I didn't know about bringing the release into the present, many more seemed inconclusive. The Karmic Board still seemed very austere and never friendly, so I didn't request their presence often.

Slightly more than a year ago, at Fall Equinox, 1995, when the Book of Life is opened, or possibly because it was my birthday, I began doing intensive karmic release work. This time the Lords of Karma came to me, demanding that I "ask" for what I needed, and that I ask again and again on a number of issues. This happened during a highly accurate psychic reading. The reader pinpointed several bits of past lives that still needed clearing. I was already aware of most of the lifetimes, and had done work to release them by other methods, but each had something more to clear, something I had missed seeing about each situation. As she spoke of each, the Lords of Karma came in and ordered me to "ask." I did, and each request to fully clear the lifetime or situation was immediately "granted."

They did not then leave as they had in the past, but remained to clear each issue the reader delineated. We were both quite amazed, but after a dozen or so of these situations released very quickly, I was afraid to continue for fear of an energy backlash that would be too intense. I decided to stop but made note of the other issues that still needed healing.

During the night, I awoke and the Lords of Karma were present. "Ask," they insisted, and I finished the list. Other than a few days of feeling very relaxed and wanting to sleep a great deal, there was no aftereffect. When I talked about it with the reader, we decided to try it for some of her healing issues, and the Lords of Karma came in and worked with her readily, also.

At this point, I decided that if these Be-ings were willing to help me I was going to keep asking until they told me to stop. Everything I cleared seemed to bring up another dozen things I wished for help with, and the four categories evolved from them. I continued to ask and was granted everything. I asked how long I could continue to do this and was told until the New Moon (they had presented themselves to me on the Full Moon). The Lords of Karma still appeared in black robes, hooded and with their faces covered, and I assumed they were all male. They would not consent to send female members of their order to work with me, and they spoke few other words than "ask," "no," or "granted." When I thanked them and asked them why they were granting me these blessings, they said "Because it's time."

It became quickly clear that anything that received a response of "granted" was healed almost immediately. Sometimes the changes happened so subtly and so easily that I didn't realize at once that they had occurred. So many things that had plagued my life simply disappeared just by asking for them. With the earlier warning to "be careful what you ask for," I devised a formula for making sure all the healings reached the present and the earthplane level (more on this in the next chapter), as my first encounter with the Lords of Karma had shown me was necessary.

As I became more familiar with working with these Beings, and they began to answer questions, I asked if I could teach others about them. I was told that people had to ask directly for themselves, but I could show them how. I tried the process with a few other people, who once they learned it were as amazed as I was, though most were more timid than I had been. When the two weeks and the New Moon passed, there was no sign of the Lords of Karma leaving or the ability to do the process ending. I asked and was told I could keep the ability until Hallows. I taught a workshop weekend in early October and was given permission to teach it to the group at the last minute. Hallows passed and I was allowed to continue. I was told I could keep it for a while and teach it; they wanted to see how people would use it. I taught it to other groups. A year later I was told that we could keep it through this lifetime and I was to write this book.

In the meantime, the Lords of Karma have changed greatly in their presence and response to me and to the others who approach them. They are now willing to talk with us (and say more than one word at a time), to lead us through the process, and give suggestions and help for achieving what we wish to heal. Their robes have changed from black to white, and the Be-ings' faces are now visible. There seem to be seven or nine Lords of Karma, though one in particular appears most clearly to me. They are not all male. They have dropped the former frightening, austere demeanor for a regal, supportive friendliness. Sometimes they even smile.

In January, 1996, I taught the karmic release process at a workshop and afterwards helped some women individually. In bed awake that night, I asked the Lords of Karma to come in so I could ask for something for myself. For the first time, they appeared to me in white robes and I could hear New Year's horns and drumming. "Hey guys," I said, "are you having a party up there? What's happening?" They replied, "It's the end of karma." I thought I hadn't heard correctly, but they repeated it. "Why?" I asked. "Critical mass," was the answer. "Because enough of us are working with you now?" I asked. They said, "Yes, because each clearing removes karma from the planet."

Apparently, each piece of individual karma is a part of the karma of the Earth. As each piece is cleared and each person healed of some past life trauma, suffering (from this or past lives), or karmic pattern, the collective mind grid of the Earth is cleared of that piece of karma, too. The Earth changes and the end of the millennium on this planet requires a full clearing and a new start, for both people and the Earth. Many of the people incarnated at this time are bodhisattvas sent back one more time for the purpose of aiding that clearing. Many others are now in their last lifetime on Earth; with the Earth changes completed the healers and troubleshooters will go elsewhere to help where they are needed. In order for people who have incarnated so often to leave Earth permanently, they must heal most or all of their still outstanding karma from their lifetimes on this planet. The planet itself must also heal Her karma to move into the New Age and complete the Earth changes. This is why the Lords of Karma have presented themselves to us now.

I once compared their presence to being turned loose in a crystal shop where everything I ever wanted was free. This is very much how it is, when the process is used ethically and with respect. Each person incarnated on Earth at this time is working out her karma in some form. With the karmic release process, the clearing becomes conscious choice and is simple enough for even children to do. If you have a realization that something is wrong in your life, you have a very good chance of being able to heal and change it. Realization is the key. We have been granted karmic grace and dispensation in this lifetime, something that may never have happened before on Earth.

The Lords of Karma are members of the angelic realm. They are angels, as our Essence and Goddess Selves are angels. Their job on the "other side" is to determine what aspects of karma are to be repeated and given a chance of healing in each lifetime, and to aid us in designing our lives accordingly. They are the most positive of Be-ings, and they direct our soul growth and evolution. No matter how austere and scary they seemed before, or how friendly they may appear now, they have been and are working for our benefit and good at all times. I have been challenged by some people who object to calling them "Lords"—the name I was first given by the healer who introduced me to them. Upon query, they are willing to be called the "Angels of Karma" or even the "Spirits of Karma," if you come to them aware of their work and who they are.

However you address them, do so with extreme respect. The warning given me was not totally facetious. These are powerful Be-ings. Ask for their presence, but do not demand it. Never argue with them and always thank them. If they tell you to do something, take them seriously. If an answer is "no," you must accept it, though there may be ways to change it. Wording is important in what you ask for, and rewording the question may give you a different answer. Do not scoff at these Be-ings, their reality, or their ability to change your life.

A friend found this out the hard way. I had taught her the process, but her life still seemed difficult. Another friend reminded her that she could go back to the Lords of Karma for help, and she said, "Lords of Karma? *What* Lords of Karma?" The two women were sitting on a screened porch in Florida. It was after 1 AM and the neighborhood and canal behind their house was totally quiet. Suddenly they saw what looked like a fireball moving across the sky, reflecting in the canal behind the porch. It seemed to come from nowhere and go nowhere, all without sound. My friend was scared speechless. The woman with her said, "You'd better apologize immediately!" She did. Another woman from the West Indies later said that on her island, karma is represented by a fireball. It was a long time before my friend was willing to speak with the Lords of Karma again, but now she does it with respect.

Some women I've taught the release process to are disturbed by the idea that the Lords of Karma are male. When I queried the Be-ings myself in the beginning, I was told I had to accept them as they were. They seemed to be all male at that time, but this is not the case. A woman at Womongathering discovered this first. She had asked for a piece of karmic release in the workshop where I taught the process. When she did, the karmic group seemed to go into conference about it, as I've sometimes seen them do. This time, however, she was shown a door opening and a woman walked into the room with the other Be-ings. The woman told the other Lords of Karma, "Give it to her, she's worked hard for it," and they did.

This was my first introduction to Nada, whom I met for myself in meditation later. She said she had been there all along, but covered by the robes they all wore. She appeared as a tall, somewhat gaunt, middle-aged woman who was obviously pregnant. As she seemed past childbearing age, I asked her about it, and she said that she was always pregnant, that "all things are born through me." Nada in Spanish means "nothing"; I had questioned her name's meaning, as well. Her explanation also explained the pregnancy. She is the Buddhist Void, the "nothing" from which all things emerge into and out of form. She is indeed the Goddess.

"Nada," in the Hindu Vedas, is the word for the sound that created the cosmos, the music of the spheres. It means spirit, creation, and the manifest and nonmanifest (visible and nonvisible, Nonvoid and Void) universe. The name is a seed sound (a bija) for the soul growth of a student and the growth of all things. All things are created by this sound, all life; all things are indeed born from Nada/nothingness. While she does not appear to me in healings or karmic release work often, her strong and gentle presence is extremely transformational when she comes. She indicated to me also that there are other women among the karmic lords, though I have not met them directly as yet.

The karmic release process with the Lords of Karma follows in the next chapter. It is simple and profound and has been given to us as a great gift. Use it well and with wisdom, and it will change and heal your life in every possible and positive way.

Karmic Release

THE KARMIC RELEASE PROCESS IS A MEDITATION, not requiring a deep trance. With experience you will be able to do it anywhere, at almost any time you can concentrate inwardly. I have taught the process to individuals and large groups. In one case, ninety women in a workshop were able to contact and work with the Lords of Karma simultaneously, everyone receiving both perception and response. Even a five-year-old child has learned the process and now uses it freely. I've been surprised to note that he has not asked for anything frivolous, not one fire truck, ant farm, or pony so far. The Lords of Karma have been very gentle with him.

To begin, enter the meditative state as in Chapter 3. Sit quietly, still your mind and take a few deep breaths. Work where you will not be interrupted and if possible where you can be alone. This is a self-healing process; no other people are required. It is important to clear your mind of extraneous thoughts so you can focus inwardly to receive the psychic impressions and information that will come.

When you are calm and feel ready, ask to speak with the Lords of Karma. You will receive some perception of them, though not everyone perceives them in the same way. You may psychically see a shadowy outline or clearer visual image of one or more of the group. Usually one member acts as spokesperson and stands out. Some visual images are symbolic; instead of pictures you may perceive light or color to represent them. You may hear their presence, as in their informing you "we are here" or "ask." My own perception of these Be-ings is most frequently by sound only; I hear them talking to me. You may feel them, as you would another person in the room, or feel sensations in any part of your body. You may feel heat, cold, or tingling without visual or other image. You may just know that they are there. Any awareness of the Lords of Karma's presence is enough.

For most people who have experienced these Be-ings, the perception is of a row of people coming into their mind or psychic vision field. They are usually robed, sometimes in black or white, or in white robes with dark collars similar to choir robes. The visual image is usually unclear, and their faces often indistinguishable. If you have trouble reaching the Lords of Karma in any other way, you may try using a pendulum for this process. Ask the pendulum if you have made the contact, and when you get a "yes" response, ask if the Lords of Karma are willing to work with you in that way. They probably will agree to do so.

Once you have some perception, any perception at all of their presence, ask for the karmic release that you wish. If your central wish is to heal a dis-ease, you may ask for it immediately, but often you will be refused until you have healed all the emotional components that go with or may be contributing to the physical condition. If you know what those emotional or mental components may be, ask for them first. These are usually anything seriously disturbing or upsetting you in your life, and they almost always involve relationships. You will not be restricted to one question, so work methodically and thoroughly and take your time. It is often best to leave your most pressing problem, especially if it is a dis-ease, for the last request at the end of the session.

You may ask for as many gifts of karmic release as you wish, but complete one before asking for the next. This is extremely important. Your questions need to be worded as simply as possible, with requests for simple "yes" or "no" answers. If you are used to working with a pendulum, this is the type of questioning to use. If you ask to heal your cancer and your relationship to your mate and your alcohol problem all in one question, you may not be able to understand the responses that come. Some of the answers may be "yes" and some "no," and some will require further work, but you won't be able to determine which is which. If you ask to heal your alcohol dependency as one question, and do the full process on the alcoholism before going to another request, you will have much better success. Take one question at a time.

Also be very careful in the wording of your question. You may be granted the request to heal the relationship with your mate, but not to heal your mate's argumentativeness. If your request is denied, try rewording it. Questions that cover the entire situation are usually more effective than those that break the problem into parts. For example, ask to heal the karma of your relationship with your mate, rather than to heal the individual things that are sources of conflict. Once the relationship has been cleared, ask at some other time for the individual things that may still remain. You'll be surprised at how few of them are left. Remember that in asking about relationships, the healing happens in you, not in the other person unless the other person also asks for it or you have her permission to ask for her. You cannot heal or change anyone's karma but your own and to try is a serious violation of universal ethics.

In asking to heal a dis-ease or condition, the wording of your request might be, "May I have karmic release from my cancer?" "May I have healing for my attention deficit disorder?" "Will you grant me karmic release for my depression?" "Will you grant me release from my smoking addiction?" Make the request very clear and very simple. For a situation or character trait, the phrasing is similar. Ask for "complete karmic release from my water phobia," or "Will you grant me release from my poverty?" or "Will you grant me the most perfect job for my needs?"

I like to ask for healing with any ongoing relationship, whether there is conflict or not, as a safeguard against later problems. For such a request, the primary way is to request "complete karmic healing for my relationship with _____." This wording can be used for almost any relationship, whether it be with a mate, child, parent, or boss. When you ask to heal a relationship you are asking to clear any negative or obstructive karma from all aspects of the relationship, and later in the process you can ask for the healing of your past lives with that person. You can also ask for karmic healing with someone no longer living, or with someone you are not currently in contact with but have had a problematic relationship with in the past.

Once in a rare while you will be directed by the Lords of Karma (or can ask them if it is appropriate) for "complete karmic severance" from a person or relationship. This is only for those people who have done you most serious harm. The request is not to be asked for or granted often. Save this one for your rapist or incest perpetrator. Ask for "complete karmic release and karmic severance from _____." First ask for karmic release with the person; then once granted, ask the Lords of Karma if severance is appropriate. Only ask for severance if the Lords of Karma indicate that they approve of the request. This can also be done with people you are shown from past lives who have done you serious harm. The harm often carries forward into the present, whether you know the person in this life or not, and may be the cause of a karmic pattern or difficulty now.

After you have made your request, wait for a response. You will perceive a "yes" or "no" in some way. You may hear the answer, or be given a visual signal. One woman sees the Lords of Karma's robes turn from black to white with a "yes," while they remain black with a "no." Another sees the sun coming out from the clouds for a "yes" and a rainstorm for "no." Other responses have included red and green traffic lights for "no" and "yes," an open highway for "yes" and an obstructed road for "no," or a rainbow for "yes" and nothing at all for "no." Sometimes the image may not be clear. Tell the Lords of Karma that you don't understand and ask for another response. One person I worked with felt "yes" as warmth in her heart center, and twinges of discomfort in her abdomen if "no." Occasionally, if the Lords of Karma decide that a request is a major breakthrough for the person asking it, they may respond by clapping, drumming, or dancing.

If the answer to your request is "yes," it is important next to bring the healing into all levels and lifetimes of your Being. This is to ensure that the healing is total. Since the wording is so important with this process, it assures that no part of what's needed for the complete karmic healing is missed or left out. Clearing a relationship in the present is important, but is not enough if the problems originated in another lifetime. The "granted" is also incomplete if the release is not brought to manifestation on the earthplane, or if its manifestation will be delayed until another lifetime. The karmic healing and release must also be brought through all the aura bodies and energy levels. Otherwise the healing of a dis-ease or manifestation of other change cannot be completed.

I discovered these things through wondering why some karmic releases that were granted manifested immediately, while others seemed not to manifest at all. The issue lies in the wording. Karma resides in the mental body and mind grid, where the whole concept of word games began. With experience, you will learn to navigate the channels of precise wording, but the following formula covers most pitfalls and activates most release processes. Here is the carefully worked out and time-tested formula. Once you receive a "yes" to your request, ask:

"May I have this healing
Through all the levels and all the bodies,
All the lifetimes including the present lifetime,
Heal all the damage (from the relationship or situation),
And bring the healing into the present NOW?"

Wait for the response. If it's "yes," the release is done. Thank the Lords of Karma and come back to now, or go to your next request.

If the answer to your original request for release has been "no," there is another part to the process. A refusal may mean that something else has to be healed before the release can be given. This is not the time to give up, and certainly not the time to argue with the Lords of Karma. Instead, try to find out what's holding up the release. Ask, "What do I need to know or do to have this healing?" and wait for the response.

You may be told to do or clear something else first, shown a past life that needs releasing, or told that the healing cannot be given at this time. Most often, you will be shown a past life or past life situation (sometimes the situation is from this life). You may or may not understand what you are being shown. Usually this type of response will be given visually. Ask for "complete karmic healing and release" from the past life or situation you are shown, whether you fully understand it or not. If you don't understand the situation, tell the Lords of Karma that you are willing to understand it. They may or may not show you further pictures.

If they say "yes" or "granted" to this request, ask for it with the above formula (through all the levels and all the bodies, etc.). If this again is a "yes," repeat your original question, the one you were refused. This time you will likely get a "yes." Ask for the release through all the levels and all the bodies..., etc. If the response is "yes" or "granted" now, you are finished. If the obstructing past life or situation *still* leaves you with another "no," ask again, "What do I need to know or do to release it?" And continue in that way.

If you continue to receive "no's," leave the question for later. After you have done other releases, and perhaps changed the wording, it may be granted. Sometimes the obstructing factor is due to other difficulties. Once they are cleared the obstruction is gone. You may not even know what the obstructing factor was. Go on to other questions, trying the one that was refused again from time to time. Also realize that some things may be karma you are not permitted to release, either at this time or in this lifetime. In my experience, however, few sincere requests remain permanently "no."

Sometimes, instead of being shown a past life as the obstructing factor when a request is denied, the Lords of Karma will direct you to do something or to work on another issue. One woman, when she asked for healing of her liver dis-ease, was told to learn to love herself more. One woman was told that her cancer would be healed when she separated from her abusive boyfriend. Another who wanted to clear a life-threatening dis-ease, was asked "Do you really wish to live?" She admitted that she wasn't sure, and was told to meditate on it and ask again when she had made her choice for continued life. One woman was told that she had a gift for healing, and would be granted her request if she agreed to develop and use her gift. Occasionally, someone is told, "We will heal this, but not at this time." A time frame may or may not be given. I've known people who forgot the exchange with the Lords of Karma entirely, but the release still happened later at the promised time.

Once you have completed one of these release processes, you may go to the next and continue with as many as you wish at one sitting. Every item you clear will remind you of many more; keep a list and work with the issues, one request at a time, until all are cleared. Don't hesitate to ask for things you feel may be impossible to heal, release, or fix. Anything is possible. It doesn't hurt to ask, and you will be totally amazed at the results.

Sometimes the "no" comes up in the last part of the process, when you ask to take the release through all the levels and all the bodies, etc. If this happens, backtrack to each phrase. Say the first line, "through all the levels and all the bodies," and ask "Can I have a 'yes' for this much of it?" If affirmative, go to the next line, and ask, "May I have it through all the lifetimes including the present lifetime?" If the response is "no," ask what you need to know or do to clear it. You will be given the information, or shown another past life or present life situation to clear. Release this as you did a "no" before, and when it becomes a "yes" go to the next line. Ask "May I heal all the damage from the situation?" If "yes," complete the request by asking, "May I bring the healing into the present NOW?" You will almost always get a "yes." At any time when you do not get a "yes," ask for further information on clearing the obstruction, clear it, then go on.

When you have been granted your full release, thank the Lords of Karma for the great gift they have offered you. Once you have received their agreement for a karmic release, it will happen at that moment, though you may feel no different. You may experience energy sensations or intense dreams that night or for a few nights (or even longer with major clearings), or you may feel or sense nothing. I call the sensations, when there are any, my molecules being rearranged and that is probably what's occurred. Often, however, you feel nothing but know that the situation has changed. When I asked to stop talking over other people, it was granted readily but I felt no different. It was only after several days that I realized I simply wasn't doing it anymore. The negative trait reappeared only once, a few months later during a migraine that lasted for several days. When I asked about it, I was told that the recurrence was neurologically based and would stop within three days; it did and has never happened again.

Most karmic releases occur immediately, but some seem to take longer, from a few days to a few months. One woman asked for help to become financially responsible in her household management. She was granted the request, and the Lords of Karma danced and drummed in delight at her asking for it. She was told, however, that the changes would come gradually over a period of six months. When we asked why, we were told that other people's karma was involved.

The information has proved to be accurate, and within the six months, noticeable changes were occurring for the woman who received the release. Sometimes a request is granted, but the release doesn't seem to happen. If it was granted, it will come in proper time for the good of all.

These karmic changes are profound in every way, even involving positive changes in your DNA and how that DNA is passed on to your children. The changes also appear in your astrological chart, as I discovered to my total amazement. I have had a visually based reading problem for most of my adult life. It comes and goes, and I have been through expensive, months-long vision therapies several times. I was having difficulty again and asked the Lords of Karma to clear it. For some weeks they refused, then finally they said "yes," but nothing seemed to shift. A week after the release I had a medical astrologer look at my chart. I have been told that the condition appears in my chart and would recur throughout this lifetime, but the astrologer (an experienced and gifted one) couldn't find it there. She said the problem was in my spine.

A month later on a workshop trip, I received a network chiropractic treatment and miraculously my reading ability returned overnight. I started going to a network chiropractor at home and my vision continued to improve. Now, every time reading becomes difficult I go to the chiropractor a couple of times and that's all it takes. It never would have occurred to me that my reading problem stemmed from my spine rather than my eyes. When you are granted a release, it is real.

This is the Lords of Karma process. It may take a few tries to get used to it, but it is simple and easy to learn. If you don't know what to do next, or how to ask, or what may need to be changed in your wording of the question, ask the Lords of Karma for help and they will give it. You cannot receive release for something you do not ask for. If you know what you need, you can probably receive help. We have been granted the ending of karma in our lifetime, and with that granted, everything is possible. As people heal their personal karma, the karma of the Earth is healed. Use the process well—and frequently. A brief outline of it is given in Appendix I.

Healing Others

THE LORDS OF KARMA PROCESS WAS DESIGNED as a self-healing tool. This is probably no accident, as so few people have access to good healers they can wholly trust and work with. Once you learn it, you will have so many things to ask for that even weekly healing sessions won't be enough. The process is primarily done alone, too, because no one but you can know what you need. Realization is crucial to the granting of karmic release and it must be self-realization; you must gain the insights to your own healing in order to be able to ask for it. You must also learn to do the asking and to know that you deserve to receive the blessings that follow—not an easy thing for many people but necessary. By being a self-healing process it also becomes a tool for empowerment, a very crucial issue for people today.

Sometimes, however, you may wish to help others who do not know the process, or who may be reluctant to (or not open to) doing it alone. The best way to work with others is to teach them to work with the Lords of Karma themselves. It is easy to give them a copy of this book. If you wish to teach someone, or use it for others in any way, first become familiar with the process by using it for yourself. When you are comfortable with working with the Lords of Karma, and you know what to do with either a "yes" or "no" response, you may wish to lead others through the process.

To do this, you may work directly with the person or on the telephone. If you are a Reiki or other hands-on healer, you may use the release process during touch healing. It also works without physical contact. Lead the karmic release in the way you would lead a meditation, first taking the person to a relaxed state, then directing her to "ask to speak with the Lords of Karma." Her perception of them may be different from yours. Just ascertain if contact has been made. Then direct her to ask her question and wait for the response.

The person asking the question will receive the psychic information, while the one leading her through the process probably will not. This means that the leader must ask the receiver to tell her when she has had a response and what it is. The receiver may not wish for the leader to know what she is asking, and that is fine. The leader needs to know only what responses are received in order to take the person to the next step. If the receiver's request is granted, the leader then asks her to repeat the formula "through all the levels and all the bodies...." line by line mentally after her. Ask for a "yes" or "no" at the end. If everything is "yes," the process can move quite quickly.

If there is a "no," tell the receiver to ask what she needs to know to clear it. Give her time to get a response, then ask her if she understands it. Lead her through releasing what she has seen, then take her back to ask once more for release of her original question. When the process is completed, ask her if she would like to be led through other questions. Continue from there. By doing this a few times, the receiver will learn the process easily. Encourage her to use it on her own.

When doing this with more than one person, the leader must make sure everyone has achieved each step before going on. Tell the group to "ask to speak with the Lords of Karma" and then wait. In a few moments, ask, "Is there anyone who has no perception of the Lords of Karma?" If someone is having difficulty, the leader must ascertain the problem. Often that person is not recognizing her perceptions as contact. When everyone has made the contact, tell the group to ask their first question, and in a few minutes more, ask "Has anyone received a 'no'?" Lead that person or persons through releasing it, then take the whole group through "all the levels and all the bodies...." If anyone gets a "no" with that, stop and lead them through clearing the problem. Timing can be a bit tricky with groups, but it will come with experience. The leader will not be given the receivers' impressions or karmic information. If someone in the group has continual difficulty with the process, work with her individually later.

I sometimes begin with a release that everyone in the group does together. Get consensus on what to ask for before beginning. One that I like to do with my women's groups is to have them all simultaneously ask the Lords of Karma for a positive self-image. Another good group release is to ask for freedom from all negative interference. Most people have some unnecessary obstacle in their lives, whether it be an attachment, energy blockage, someone jealous of them, outright psychic attack, or alien energy implant. This karmic clearing can have immediately freeing results for many people. Suspect negative interference especially when someone says her psychic abilities suddenly disappeared some time ago, or that suddenly everything is going wrong in her life. Energy balancing can also do wonders for this; see the rest of this book.

You may try other group karmic releases if there is consensus on what to ask for. After a few of these, ask the group to ask individually to heal a problematic relationship—everyone has one or several dozen of these. Then ask them to clear a situation or character trait they wish to change. Finally, ask them to request healing for a dis-ease or condition. By the time you have led the group through several karmic releases, everyone will have learned the process and be able to do it for themselves from then on.

People being led through this process must do their own asking for release. If they do not ask the Lords of Karma themselves, they will not be granted the karmic clearing. No one can do this for someone else, with the exception of someone asking for karmic healing for a small child. In this case, the child's parent may do the process by first asking permission for it from the Lords of Karma. To do this, have your child at rest or asleep and place your hands on his or her body. If the child is old enough to be verbal, ask her participation—you will be amazed at how well even very young children can work with you. If old enough, the child can do the asking, with the parent telling her what to ask for. Children see Be-ings like the Lords of Karma readily and will be glad to talk with them themselves. Ask the Lords of Karma to come in, and then ask the child's Higher Self, spirit guides, and guardian angels to join the healing.

Next ask the Lords of Karma if the healing or release you wish for is for the child's best good. If they agree, ask them for it or have the child ask them. If the child is too young to participate, the parent will receive the information. If the child is older, the parent may receive the information along with the child, or the child may perceive it alone. Do the process in the same way as you would with yourself or another adult, having the child participate as much as possible. If a "no" response must be released, ask the Lords of Karma to release it in the same way you would for yourself. When you get a "yes," ask for it through "all the levels and all the bodies...," as you would in any other release process.

Children will surprise and amaze you. I have taught the process to a twelve-year-old who quickly learned it and uses it as well and as responsibly as any adult. The Lords of Karma will be gentle with children, and if the child asks for something inappropriate she will be directed to what she really needs. I did the process with a five-year-old who amazed me even more. Josh had been having too much trouble in kindergarten and his mother asked me to find out why and help him. She put her hands on the child in bed, and I sat at the foot of the bed and led them through it. First we asked to speak to the Lords of Karma, but Josh made us wait until his angels came in. He knew exactly when that was, and could see the Lords of Karma visually as well. He told us where they were, how many, what they looked like, and he talked to them throughout.

We asked for several behavioral changes, which both Josh and the Lords of Karma agreed to, and they were granted. We asked that the boy learn to be very good in school, that he stop hitting or hurting other children, that he learn when to be quiet, and that he be very good at obeying his teacher. When his mother and I ran out of ideas, we asked Josh if he had other things to ask for. I expected silly things but was totally surprised. He asked to know when he was hurting someone else, because he really wasn't sure when he was doing it and didn't want to hurt anyone. He also asked, and scared his mother badly, "not to hurt himself on purpose." He may have done just that in a past life, and now used the session to accomplish a major karmic clearing for this lifetime. From the time of the karmic release session, his teacher's reports improved greatly and he became much quieter at school and at home.

One further thing his mother asked for was that Josh go to bed at night without a fuss. The typical bedtime routine was of Josh bouncing in and out of bed like a yo-yo until eleven o'clock or later. His mother was not pleased. We asked that he "go to sleep as soon as he goes to bed every night and have wonderful dreams." We convinced Josh to ask for it, too—he liked the idea of the dreams. The Lords of Karma agreed. From that night on, the child has gone to bed at eight o'clock and stayed there. He no longer fusses all night and he tells his mother about his dreams in the morning.

Animals can be healed in similar ways. The Lords of Karma are willing to work with them, and when I asked about it they informed me that pets have both souls and karma. Pick a time when the animal is quiet or asleep. Sit beside her, put your hands on her body, and ask to speak with the Lords of Karma. If you have psychic communication with the pet, ask her to participate; some will do so. Ask permission from the Lords of Karma for the healing you intend, and they will tell you "yes" or "no." Ask for what you wish for the animal, and do the process as you would for a child. The Lords of Karma will tell you what you need to know.

From the response of my dogs with this, I believe they also receive pictures or impressions. The karmic releases for a pet will mainly be about your relationship with the animal, or about healing dis-eases, conditions, or negative behaviors. If your dog or cat was an animal shelter rescue or if you suspect other past abuse, ask to heal and clear it. When you do karma work for yourself, don't forget to ask for karmic healing for *your* relationship with the animal if there are difficulties in it. I have seen some improvements and changes in working with pets, but they are not as conclusive as with people. There may be more we need to know about this work between humans and animals.

For advanced healers and those very experienced with the process, karmic release can be done at a distance as a psychic healing. This is not to be done often or lightly, but only when there is real need and no way to work with the person directly. Be very careful of ethics if you choose to do this. The risk for harm here is to yourself—you will not be permitted to wrongly influence or manipulate others. If you attempt to manipulate someone else even "for their own good," however, the consequences are your own and they are serious. With that warning in mind, I will describe the process of doing karmic release at a distance ethically.

First, ask to speak with the Lords of Karma, tell them what you wish to request for the other person and ask their permission to do it. If they agree, ask the person's Higher Self to join the Lords of Karma with you. The Lords of Karma may not agree to the healing until the person's Higher Self is present. You need to be in a deeper than usual trance state for this, and your impressions will probably be visual. You will see the Lords of Karma and the other person, or some representation of her. Ask the person's Higher Self if she is willing to accept the karmic release you wish to ask for. If she agrees to it, and only if she agrees, ask the Lords of Karma for the release. Do it from this point in the same way you would do a karmic release for yourself. When you have completed the work you wish to do, thank the Lords of Karma and the person's Higher Self, and return to now.

You may occasionally be permitted to do karmic healing for another in this way. For some requests you will be told that the person has to ask for it consciously. For others, the requests will be granted easily. If at all possible and as soon as possible, repeat the release with the person's conscious participation. Only do healing in this way if there is no other option and the release seems clearly and immediately needed. I have worked with another woman to do such releases for a mutual friend. The woman wants the healing, but is difficult to catch for direct work. We keep a list of what we have asked for, reading it to her the next day by telephone, and then repeat the list consciously when we can. She has agreed to the process, and thanks us for it. Her continuing healing is apparent in her actions and her life. Do karmic release of this type only very carefully, however.

The chapters that follow contain techniques for core soul healing directed by the Lords of Karma.

PART II

Energy Balancing

Ascension and the Higher Self

A LARGE PART OF THE INTENT OF KARMIC release is to heal all the damage from all our many lifetimes on Earth. This includes damage to the energy bodies, templates, personality "selves," chakras, and the rest of the human energy system that comprises who we are. Once you have learned to remove the karmic obstructions from your physical and near-to-physical bodies, this is the next step. Most karmic release healing takes place in the mental body and mind grid, and affects the mental, emotional, etheric, and physical levels. In our many incarnations, however, we may have received energy damage farther out. The Etheric Double and Astral Twin are easily damaged, and the mind grid, spiritual body, and causal body can also be. This damage is a less apparent and more technical part of human karma, and it is also less easily healed.

While the Essence Self and Goddess Self cannot be harmed by incarnational wear and tear, the templates at all levels can be damaged, closed, and are often misaligned. The chakras of the hara and kundalini lines also may need healing and alignment. One or more of the energy bodies may not be operating optimally. Though much of our energy system is self-healing, where the damage is more than superficial, the healing often does not happen completely. We have been in bodies many, many times on Earth and on other planets, and have experienced every sort of trauma and suffering. Most of us are exhausted to the soul, and lack the extra nonphysical energy to self-heal completely. Often this damage requires work at levels most people are not consciously aware of. Attention deficit disorder, multiple personality disorder, cancer, some genetic dis-eases, and depression are examples of probable energy damage at the outer aura levels or to the personality "selves."

In addition, the energy shifts of planet Earth during the current Earth changes have created even more challenges to our lives and energy bodies. Some twin souls, true soul mates, expecting to be together in this lifetime were damaged by Earth energy aberrations at the time of this incarnation. Instead of being with our soul mates in this lifetime, the damage caused rupture in our joinings and unions, and much heartache. I often hear examples of a woman who knows who her mate is, but the other person will not recognize her or consider their relationship. The woman knows that she has been with this person through many lifetimes and cannot understand the mate's nonrecognition or vacillating attitude now. I experience this in my own life. Couples born from about 1946 to 1966 have been especially affected. We have been promised by the Lords of Karma that through karmic grace and the Earth changes, this damage will be healed, and we will be reunited with our true mates in this lifetime.

The planet and people are also experiencing major and disrupting energy shifts in an ongoing way. Earth's entrance into the influence of the photon belt, a band of transformative energy, has already happened, and its effects will continue increasingly until 2013. This energy field is creating havoc with mechanical objects like airplane guidance systems and promoting change in people's emotions and thought forms. The photon belt's escalation of human vibrational energy has resulted also in increasing psychic ability that may be disturbing to some people. We are being forced to be all that we can be by this energy, and this is not bad, but the changes may be intensive. The planet's vibration is increasing along with ours. Earth has left the third dimension and is now traversing the fourth. We will soon move into the fifth dimension, beyond which karma does not exist. These shifts have brought the Lords of Karma to us, with their karmic grace and release, and though much of Earth's energy is disruptive now, most of the changes are ultimately positive.

One of Earth's less positive changes happened recently. In September, 1996, just about the time that the planet Mercury went retrograde for three weeks, as it does about three times a year, Earth also went retrograde momentarily. This is something that astrologically has never happened before and it happened as a lesser of two evils. Had it not, there would have been catastrophic planetary disasters with major loss of life.

Nevertheless, with Earth retrograded, every negativity on the planet seemed to be released. Energy damage to our etheric and emotional bodies, as well as to our kundalini and hara line chakras, occurred severely in some people, mostly those who are psychically sensitive. The negative effects continued for the rest of 1996. For those people whose lives in September suddenly turned nightmarish, this is the explanation. Most of the energy damage from this period has now been cleared, but there is still much to be healed for people on Earth. While some of this incarnational damage is repaired in the between-life state, most damage that occurs while incarnated can be healed only while we are in physical bodies.

Another factor of the Earth changes is what some psychics call ascension. There have been many wild stories about this one, to the effect that hundreds or thousands of us will disappear in one day, in three separate waves. Those that do will find themselves on a spaceship, while their families will have no idea where they've gone. This isn't exactly the case. In my understanding, ascension is the ultimate goal of karmic release and karmic grace. Once we have cleared most or all of our still remaining past life suffering and energy damage, we are freed from the Wheel of Incarnation. We no longer have to reincarnate since we have learned what we needed to from the process and can now evolve further. As I mentioned previously, many of those in service to the planet in this lifetime will no longer reincarnate here, and must clear their remaining karma with the Earth and Earth incarnation.

Ascension means that when we die, we will no longer reenter the process of rebirth. The exception to this may be those who choose to return to help others, the bodhisattvas, many of whom are incarnated here now for the Earth changes. By releasing our karma with the aid of the Lords of Karma process and in other ways, we clear our own and the planet's mind grid (Earth grid) of karma as well. The Earth, and eventually all who live here, will also no longer be subject to karma or involuntary rebirth. Karma is not a part of planetary organization or law beyond the fourth dimensional energy vibration, and Earth is reaching the fifth dimension through the Earth changes now. By having cleared our Earth Akashic Record, and by having cleared the planet's karma through our service to Her, we may now stop incarnating and evolve further elsewhere. Many healers and teachers are having their last incarnation on Earth. If we incarnate again, we will do so on other planets. Earth incarnations are considered to be more difficult than most others and having saved this planet from destruction (or at least done our best) we are nearly finished here.

But what's all this about a spaceship? Many people dream of the ships and a few are privileged to see them. They are the collection points for souls who have died and will no longer reincarnate on this planet. From the ships we will be taken home to our planets of origin, with our mates and soul families. None of us originated on Earth; everyone who lives here was brought here from somewhere else. Most of us came from one of the planets in the Pleiadian Federation, and a few souls originated in the Sirius or Orion star systems. If you have had dreams of being with others in a somewhat seedy recreation room, with paneled walls, linoleum floors, and tacky 1950s plastic furniture you have been on the ships! They are not scary at all, but they do need a decorator. You may have had dreams or visions of living in a grey, carpet-walled room like a narrow cubicle—these are the bedrooms on the ships. If your dreams have been about elevators or you sometimes feel like you are "falling up" (or down) as you go into or come out of sleep, you have been to the ships in your dreamtime. Dreams of being at a school or university may also be of the ships, or may be dreams of going home. Some of them may be memories of the between-life state.

We will not go to the ships in other than our dreams until we die at the normal ending of our lifetimes. They are our vehicles for the trip home to our planets of origin, something to celebrate. We are not going to disappear en masse one day or be abducted by aliens. When we go to the ships and arrive home, we will be fully conscious. However, we can go only if we have cleared our Earth karma and repaired the damage to our energy systems and core souls accrued from living on Earth for so many lifetimes. To do this ascension in a fully conscious way, we must also activate and be reconnected with our personality "selves," particularly our Higher Self. Her energy must be brought into our nearer-to-physical aura bodies, where she will complete the healing for our Astral Twin and Etheric Double and merge with them.

Once this has happened, the Higher Self becomes strong enough to receive the energy, again into our closer-to-physical bodies, of our Essence/Star Selves. The Essence Self is our Akashic Record and her activation at nearer-to-physical conscious levels completes the clearing of our karma and the healing of all the energy damage of the many incarnations.

The last process is the activation of our Goddess Self/Oversoul. She may be brought in to join and merge with the Essence Self, and with her comes the awareness of who we truly are as souls and members of an intergalactic community of many planets and galaxies. Full connection with the Goddess may then also follow. For all our many lifetimes on Earth we have been separated from these parts of who we are, and we can now be reunited. People on Earth have been cut off from most of our Be-ing, but this is ready to change.

A further aspect of energy balancing, karmic release, and ascension is that of healing our DNA. Human DNA is much more than the two strand double helix we have been taught. Our DNA consists of twelve strands, ten of which were deactivated at some point in Earth herstory, probably much more recently than we realize. My guess is that it coincided with the patriarchal takeover of the Goddess matriarchies in Old Testament times. With the loss of the full complement of active DNA, we lost our psychic abilities, our realization of who we are, and our realization of and interaction with other planetary civilizations. We lost awareness of our outer "selves" and energy bodies. Much of the damage to human energy has been the result of the damage to our DNA, which is said to contain the genetics for all the life forms of the universe, a "living library." The deactivation was done to us during a war between planets for control of our destinies. For a time the bad guys won, and the battles still go on, but good will prevail. Now is the time for our DNA to be repaired, our energy restored, karma cleared, and for our full understanding of who we really are.

The energy balancing process that begins in the next chapter is a step in this healing and restoration. It was given to me piece by piece after the September, 1996, Earth retrograde, as I was working to heal my own severe energy damage from that time. I work directly with the Lords of Karma and with Brede, the planetary guardian now manifesting frequently on Earth. She is the Celtic Maiden Goddess Brigit, lately assumed to be Mary, who is the Lady appearing at Medjugorje and a number of other places on several continents, including Clearwater, Florida. Her picture is on the cover of my book *Psychic Healing with Spirit Guides and Angels*. In one of my healing meditations I was directed by Brede to ask the Lords of Karma for a series of items, step by step, most of which I didn't understand at the time. The results were so healing, comforting, and joyful that I wrote the sequence down and began using it for others. It has taken me some time to understand just what the steps meant and what they accomplish. Additions to the process came as I was ready to receive them, over a period of four months.

By doing this energy balancing process, you will feel more present, whole, and stable on the Earth and in your daily life. It clears energy disruptions and repairs and aligns the whole energy system. Your mind will be clearer and your emotions more stable and calm. Your life purpose will be more available to you and easier to accomplish. There is a great sense of relief, peace, and joy with this process, a wellness that seems to be permanent and that requires only a little follow-up. It will also teach you, as it did me, the mechanics of our energy systems and the magick of who we are beyond the little we know of our physical bodies. Most healers have some awareness of our nearer-to-physical levels, but not the levels beyond them. The energy balancing process gives new understanding of the closer levels, and an introduction to the ones that are further away.

Bringing in one's Higher Self is a direct route to healing our Astral Twin inner child. This means the healing of all damage to our child-selves, whether the damage be from incest or abuse or from simply growing up and having to put aside that part of who we are. The Astral Self is our joy in living and we need her back fully healed. The Higher Self's merging into and joining with the Astral Twin also heals the Etheric Double, the subconscious infant-self who holds our fears and who may have wants that seem inexplicable to the adult. Recurrent nightmares may disappear with this, along with one's fearfulness of others and distrust of life. With the entrance of the Higher Self, we heal our inner infant and child, and gain access to the Maiden Goddess of our Be-ing.

Bringing in one's Essence Self, the Mother, occurs in a later chapter. She is the nurturing aspect of our Be-ing, our ability to take care of ourselves and others in a mature and competent way. The Essence Self contains memory of all our lifetimes, our full Akashic Record, and retains the experience of all we have learned in those incarnations. She knows how to do things we cannot do, as does our Higher Self, so if you need help with something in your life you may ask for the assistance and input of both. While the Higher Self is wonderful at healing, calming, and at aiding earthplane problems, the Essence Self can help with karmic energy difficulties that seem unresolvable. She is both healer and soul mechanic. She is also an angel, and angels have great reputations as protectors, and at manifesting miracles and gifts in human life. Remember also that she is you. She is gentle, joyful, and very strong.

One's Goddess Self/Oversoul is the last "self" to bring into your nearer-to-physical energy. How to do this is described later also. When the Goddess Self comes into your energy, she will join and merge with your Essence Self. The Essence Self, in turn, has joined and merged with your Higher Self, and the Higher Self has joined and merged with the Astral Twin. The Astral Twin, with the help of the Higher Self, joins and merges with the Etheric Double that directly interfaces the physical body and physical consciousness. As these energies integrate with each other and affect the physical, your life may change deeply for the better. One almost immediate result of bringing in your Goddess Self is a gradual decrease and disappearance of depression. You will feel more at home on Earth, and more able to function optimally here despite the difficulties of this Earth change incarnation and the frequent planetary energy shifts. Ask your Goddess Self for what you wish for most. She is the wisdom of the Crone, the all-knowing and all-giving grandmother. She is you, and is transcendent ecstatic joy.

Your Goddess Self is not the Goddess, but once she is merged with your other energy "selves," the Goddess can be invited in. Just as your Essence Self joins a group of other Essence Selves to form an Oversoul (Goddess Self), a collection of twenty to forty Oversouls joins together, under the care of a Goddess. The Goddess name you have been most consciously attracted to or aware of is probably the Goddess you will meet when you invite Her to merge with your energy and other "selves." The experience of this merging can only be described as pure light.

Energy Balancing also repairs and reconnects our DNA and accomplishes core soul healing. By core soul healing I mean the repair, replenishment, alignment, and activation of the optimal energy function of all the bodies and all the component parts of who we are. The template hatchways between the bodies, which give access and energy flow from one level to the next, are cleared and activated. The chakras are cleared and aligned and their functions repaired and balanced. While this all sounds complex—and it is—the process is simple, gentle, and safe. I have done it on myself, many other adults, on five-year-old Josh (who loved it), and on my dogs. Copper informed me that he had already done it a few times, while Kali was in bliss. Most people experience bliss with this process—it brings an ongoing joyful transcendence into our lives, a boost we need badly at this time, a salve to the soul level exhaustion so many people are experiencing.

The basic energy balancing meditation is given in the next chapter, with more information on how to use it after. Later chapters include bringing in one's Essence and Goddess Selves, one's personal Goddess, and information on using it to clear and align the hara and kundalini chakras. Even if you don't understand the soul mechanics of the process, do it anyway, and let it take its beneficial course. You don't have to know what it means to enjoy it.

The Energy Balancing Process

LIKE THE PROCESS OF WORKING WITH THE Lords of Karma, the energy balancing process is a meditation. You will need to be more relaxed for it than for karmic work, however, and it is probably best experienced lying down. The basic process below takes about half an hour to complete, and you will not wish to be interrupted during it. Afterwards, you may want to stay with the energy and your Higher Self a little longer, and you are welcome to do so. Upon getting up from the meditation, you will find that you are not spacy and you feel very well. You will feel grounded, calm, and joyful. Discussion on how to keep this well-being permanently follows in later chapters, as well as information for even more energy healing.

When doing this process it is extremely important to do each step in sequence. The Lords of Karma will not grant a go-ahead to any step that is out of the designated order. It is also important to go through each step completely before asking for the next one. You will feel energy sensations with each step as soon as you ask for it to happen. Relax with the energy until it stops, and do not go further until the energy process at each level is complete. The sensations last for approximately five minutes at each step, with DNA reconnection possibly lasting longer. The request for complete core soul healing will be granted in the meditation, but its effects will continue for some time after it. Go to the next step in the process as soon as the energy sensations end.

The sensations you experience may be different from any you have had before. You may see colors and light patterns, spinning wheels, spirals, geometric figures, or rainbows. The colors may not be those you know in the Earth spectrum. You may feel heat or cold, water flowing through your body, or energy sensations that seem to proceed fairly rapidly from head to feet. (When they reach your feet they are usually finished, and so is that step in the sequence.) You may hear music or smell flowers. When your Higher Self enters you will feel her, hear her, be able to talk with her, and may see her. Later, when you bring in your Essence Self, you are even more likely to have a visual image. You may experience images and sensations you have never perceived before, but all of them will be pleasant. You will feel a great sense of both excitement and peace throughout the process.

To begin, first find a comfortable place to lie down. You may do this in bed if you can keep from falling asleep there, but a soft rug on the floor may be more ideal. Do this at a time when you are alone and will not be interrupted, and take the phone off the hook. The process can also be done as a group meditation, but in working with a group make sure everyone has completed each step before moving to the next. Also, the leader should have already completed her energy balancing, as she will not be able to lead it and do it at the same time. She should be familiar with the process and what happens at each step. If working alone, you may keep the outline of the process with you (see Appendix II) to refer to along the way. Taping the meditation is less effective, unless you can turn the tape on and off while waiting for each step to finish. Energy balancing is best done by those who are experienced at working with the Lords of Karma.

Lie down and get comfortable. You may wish to remove your shoes and loosen belts. Take a few moments to relax and do a few deep breaths. Calm your body and your thoughts. When you are ready to begin, *ask to speak with the Lords of Karma*. You will perceive them as you do when doing other karmic energy work. This time, however, when you make your request the process will happen immediately, unless you receive a "no" response. You will not hear "yes" or "granted." If you receive a "no" at any time, stop the energy balancing process, and ask what you need to do to release the "no" before going on. This seldom happens if you take the steps in correct sequence. On the one occasion that it has, the woman was told to gain karmic release for a rape she had been victim of in this lifetime. When she asked for it, and for release and karmic severance from her rapist, she was granted the requests and then allowed to complete the energy balancing.

For the first step, ask the Lords of Karma to *align all of your energy bodies and the connections between the energy bodies.* Use my wording precisely for these requests, as I have experimented with various wordings to discover what works best. Unless you hear a "no" response, the energy sensations will begin, often before you have even finished asking. Lie quietly and appreciate the sensations for as long as they last. Keep your mind clear and do not try to analyze what's happening. Remain still until the sensations stop. You may then go to the next step in the process.

The energy bodies are meant to be in alignment with one another. When they are not, and they shift out of sequence fairly easily, energy flows and information are obstructed from one level to the next. I have had difficulty for much of my life with a lot of chatter in my mind. Sometimes it became disturbing and even frightening, and nothing I did ever eased or stopped it for long. This first request of the energy balancing process completely stopped it. If it starts to return, I simply ask to align the bodies again and it goes away. This was the beginning of my energy balancing work, and initially the only step. It is a highly important one.

When the body alignment is completed, ask the Lords of Karma to *clear, heal, align, open, and activate your Ka Template.* Again wait for the sensations to stop before going on. The Ka Template is an energy hatchway that connects your physical body to the etheric body level. It connects directly through your root (kundalini) and perineum (hara line) chakras. Requests to heal the templates usually happen immediately and proceed rapidly, as long as they are kept in sequence.

When the sensations finish, go to the next of the five templates and make the same request. Ask the Lords of Karma to *clear, heal, align, open, and activate your Etheric Template.* Sensations will begin again. Wait until they stop before going on. The Etheric Template connects the etheric body to the emotional/astral body, through the heart (kundalini) and thymus (hara line) chakras. Remember that the back of the heart chakra is the attachment site of the Sliver Cord where the personality "selves" and Goddess connect to each other and the body. This is a very important template that needs healing in most people.

Next, ask the Lords of Karma to *clear, heal, align, open, and activate your Ketheric Template.* You will feel a new set of sensations. Wait until they stop before going on. The Ketheric Template connects the emotional to the mental body, through the kundalini third eye and the hara line causal body chakras. This is your entrance into the mind grid and to all karmic clearing and release. This template connects our minds to our emotions and then our emotions to our bodies.

When the sensations stop, ask the Lords of Karma to *clear, heal, align, open, and activate your Celestial Template.* Experience the new sensations, which may be more intense at this level. The Celestial Template connects the mental to the spiritual body, also connecting the crown (kundalini) and transpersonal point (hara line) chakras. The spiritual body is the access to your Higher Self, and the Celestial Template must be cleared and activated for Higher Self, Essence Self, or Goddess Self to enter. Wait for the sensations to subside before going on. They may take a little longer than the sensations of the earlier templates.

Next, ask the Lords of Karma to *clear, heal, align, open, and activate your I-Am Template.* The sensations with this opening may be very intense, and you may feel uncomfortable in your throat chakra for a few minutes after doing it. The I-Am Template connects your spiritual body to the lower causal body level. There are no hara or kundalini line chakra connections, as this template is beyond the closer-to-physical energy levels entirely. This is the connecting access of the nearer-to-physical bodies to your Essence/Star Self, and its clearing is necessary to be able to bring her energy into your consciousness.

It took a five-year-old to discover this template for me. I had done the Lords of Karma session and energy balancing (as far as I knew it at that time) with Josh. When his mother and I finished, or thought we had finished, and left the child to go to sleep, he called us back. "You forgot a 'temple'," he said. I asked him to tell me more about it, and he said it was the "I-Am temple." We went back to the Lords of Karma, verified its presence, and asked for its healing in Josh. Then I had to try it for myself. Clearing at this level is a major spiritual opening. When doing energy balancing with a small child, you will clear the templates, but probably not bring in the child's Higher Self. Ask the Lords of Karma for direction.

Stay with this energy for a few minutes, and when the sensations shift again, ask the Lords of Karma to *reconnect, heal, and activate your twelve-strand DNA.* Reconnecting is not enough, the connections must also be healed and made active. This step in the sequence takes longer than the others, and the sensations may be the most interesting. Several people have reported seeing a spinning double helix and feeling like they were spinning with it. There may be lots of lights and fireworks. The activation takes only a few minutes, but it has karmic and lifelong consequences that we may only imagine at this point. This is an important step in human energy evolution, and it may leave you feeling a bit dizzy or giddy for a while. You may hear the Lords of Karma clapping when you ask for this.

Next, ask the Lords of Karma for *complete core soul healing*. This covers all of the energy levels and the nonphysical anatomy of all the bodies, as far out as the core soul/Goddess Self. Its purpose is to cover any needed healing that may have been missed in karmic release or any other healing process, including the energy balancing so far. It includes healing damage to any of the personality "selves," templates, energy bodies, Sliver Cord, and chakras.

A number of other processes can be requested here, and I will discuss them in the next chapter. Most of them are aimed at further and more specific core soul healing work and energy clearing. Wait to do them until the next time you do the energy balancing process. This is to keep the process as simple as possible for your first experience with it. Also, energy balancing is quite intense, and limiting it now makes the additions later much easier to handle.

When the sensations have again stopped, *ask your Higher Self to come in*. You will feel her energy enter, and it may proceed from head to feet. While the feeling is ecstatic, and you may feel filled with light, you may or may not receive a visual picture of what your Higher Self looks like. Once the sensations of her entering are complete, *ask her name.* Some people get this on the first try, but others do not receive their Higher Self's name until the second or third time they bring her energy in. Wait a moment to try and hear the name, but whether you receive it or not, go on.

Next, *ask your higher self for a gift and she will ask a gift of you.* Mine came in telling me what her gift to me would be before I could ask, and when I offered her a gift in return, she asked to be given all my pain. Others' gifts have been reunions with their soul mates, the finding of their life purpose, the healing of a dis-ease, peace of mind, joy, or happiness. Higher Selves have asked to receive their person's pain, grief, worry, or poverty. Let her tell you what she wants for her gift. You will be offered something you have always wanted, and asked for something you would like to lose. You will gain both ways and feel as if a heavy weight has been lifted from your soul, as if you finally have help and aren't alone.

Invite your Higher Self to connect with you and remain within your consciousness permanently. This will not happen immediately; you will need to bring your Higher Self's energy in daily for a while to make it happen. This can take as long as several months for some people or only a week or two for others. More on this in the discussion of follow-up later.

Ask your Higher Self to clear, heal, align, open, activate, and fill your hara line chakras and energy channels. This brings your Higher Self firmly into your emotional/astral body energy and connects her fully with your Astral Twin, who resides on the emotional body level. Your Higher Self will do whatever healing your Astral Twin requires. The hara line is the Astral Twin's energy system and her access to the etheric body and Etheric Double. This part of the process will take five or ten minutes, and you will feel the energy move from your head to your feet vertically. When it reaches your feet, go on to the next request.

Ask your Higher Self to clear, heal, align, open, activate, and fill your kundalini line chakras and energy channels. The energy moves downward horizontally, in a spiral from side to side. The request gives the Higher Self access through the hara line and Astral Twin to the etheric body and Etheric Double. She may then complete the healing of these levels. The etheric chakras are the kundalini chakras, the ones closest to the physical body. Healing this energy system and the infant-self Etheric Double may also provide physical body healing. Whether it does or not, this step will provide a great feeling of well-being. It completes the connection of the Higher Self into physical consciousness.

To finish the basic energy balancing, now ask of the Lords of Karma and your Higher Self that *all the processes and alignments just completed become permanent.* They will not become permanent immediately, but this request will help to make them eventually permanent, or almost so. Templates in particular seem to shift at times, and the energy bodies may need occasional realignment. The DNA activation and request for core soul healing need to be done only once. You will wish to ask your Higher Self, however, to come in often. To do so without other energy balancing, enter the meditative state, then ask her to clear and activate the Ka Template, and then come in. It is not necessary to do the rest of the energy balancing to bring in your Higher Self. If you cannot reach your Higher Self by doing this, ask the Lords of Karma first to align all the energy bodies, then clear all the templates, each in turn, and try again.

Once you have stayed with your Higher Self and talked with her for a while, *come back to now* and end the meditation. The basic energy balancing process is finished. An easy-to-follow outline of it is found in Appendix II.

Energy Balancing and Core Soul Healing

THE ENERGY BALANCING OF THE LAST CHAPTER can be extended to a variety of core soul healing processes, most of them based on your increased understanding of soul structure. To use it in this way, repeat the energy balancing process, but in place of the requests for DNA reconnection and complete core soul healing, add some of the items listed below. DNA reconnection needs to be done only once, as does your request for core soul healing—which will continue automatically for some time after you ask for it. Most of the suggestions below also need to be done only once or, at least, very infrequently. However, where you are asking to clear and heal energy bodies, energy flows, the Sliver Cord, or chakras, you may wish to repeat the healing about once a week.

You may make a few of these requests in one meditation, but be careful not to overload. The changes being asked for are profound, despite the simplicity of the process. They will cause major shifts in your soul structure and in your life. While all of the changes and healing are positive in every way, the energy shifts can feel disruptive while they are happening. You may feel drained, tired, or spacy while the changes are taking place, and this may last from a few days to a few weeks after each session. You may also experience some symptoms of physical detoxification, like diarrhea, nausea, frequent urination, body odor, or a runny nose for about a week. Drink lots of water and treat yourself gently. You may feel vulnerable and wish to withdraw from crowds and hectic activities for a while. None of these symptoms are harmful, and they will pass. Do not use medication to stop the detox process; what is clearing is for your own good.

Wait until the detoxification and changes stop before continuing your energy balancing meditations. How frequently you do this work is highly individual, go with how you feel and when you are ready. A pendulum can help you determine when to continue. A pendulum may also help you to understand which of the following items are useful for your own needs. You may also ask the Lords of Karma about each one. Not everyone will need everything here, but most people will benefit from the full list. Take the items slowly, and appreciate the transformation and healing they offer to your life.

Begin with the energy balancing process of the last chapter. Ask to speak with the Lords of Karma. Ask them to align your energy bodies. Ask them to clear, heal, align, open, and activate all five templates (Ka, Etheric, Ketheric, Celestial, and I-Am). Do the items from the list that you have chosen for the day; three or four are probably enough. Then ask your Higher Self to come in. Direct her to clear, heal, align, open, activate, and fill first the hara line channels and chakras, and then the kundalini. Ask her help in completing the healing you have done in this session, and ask that the positive changes become permanent and self-maintaining. Finally, ask for a comfortable and easy integration of the changes (this may prevent a lot of symptoms), and come back to now.

First on the list is something I use in groups to teach people to work with the Lords of Karma, but it may work better for energy balancing. Ask to *release from your energy all manipulation and negative interference*. We have come through many lifetimes on a planet that has been subjected to every sort of manipulation, and most people have experienced too much of it. Manipulation is presented to us every day on the TV news, and it occurs just as often on the personal level. Negative interference can mean any of a number of things, from alien implants (not a fantasy) to psychic attacks from a jealous coworker. Interference or manipulation can originate in this lifetime or be left over from past lives. Your request may also clear interference to your energy from the vibrational changes of the planet. Remember that damage to your energy and aura bodies remains until it is cleared. Now is the time, and this is the opportunity to clear it.

You may be surprised at how this request can change your life, and I recommend everyone to ask for it. If your psychic abilities seem to have suddenly disappeared, or if you feel you have never had them, this may be the cure. If you feel that your life is out of control and that nothing you do turns out right, this may also be the cure. If you have been repeatedly ill, depressed, suicidal, or exhausted, this is a good place to start to change it. Women have come to me for healing, saying that they feel blocked in some aspect of their life or in one of the chakras. I take them through this release immediately.

You may also ask to be *released, cleared and healed from all energy of psychic attacks in all your bodies and levels.* These may be from this life or other lifetimes, and we all have experienced them. Some were intentional, and may have been very nasty, while others were simply bad thoughts or bad vibes from others. I did a lecture tour some years ago and a group of "born-again" Christian women followed me from one venue to the next. They informed me that they were praying for my death. Within a few days I developed the flu, which made the rest of the trip very difficult. I also developed a fear of lecturing that took several years to clear. My vision difficulties kicked in with a yearlong vengeance: they had repeatedly pressured me with the question, "If you can heal yourself, why do you wear eyeglasses?" I felt exhausted, depressed, and sick for a long time after the trip. I had long-term negative emotional effects from it.

Years later a healer found what we interpreted to be a psychic attack implanted in my solar plexus. It looked like a barbed arrow with a string attached, and the chakra around it was ripped and festered. She asked me where it had came from, and the Christians immediately came to mind. I hadn't thought of them in a very long time. The healer determined that the attack had been sent consciously and was still being renewed and activated. When she removed it, and we broke the chakra cords to the sender, I was nauseous and sick for about a week, then began to feel much better. I lost my stage fright, gained energy, and felt much calmer and safer. Years later still, when I asked the Lords of Karma to clear me of all negative interference, they showed me a piece of the arrow still imbedded on a deeper level not reached in the healing, and they removed it.

Unlike the above, most psychic attacks are indirect. The person sending it may be negative toward you and wish you harm, but probably does not realize they are actually attacking you. Jealous and angry people are prone to do this, and those who wish they could control or manipulate you. Negative people of this sort that you have refused to accommodate are likely perpetrators of indirect attacks. Some psychic attacks are more desperate than negative. An emotionally needy person may cling to you and drain your energy, consciously or not, because she feels she can't cope on her own. You may feel tired or not quite well because of the energy drain, but the person usually has no idea she is harming you and really no intention to. Any of these situations may have happened in this lifetime, or be left over from past lives. Someone who has attacked you with intent in this lifetime may also have attacked you before.

In a similar healing, *ask to be cleared and released from all attachments, negative entities, and elementals.* Attachments are negative, other-dimensional, nonhuman Be-ings, and everyone incarnates with some of them in their energy. When released, they may look like grotesques or "monsters," and in psychic healing they are sent to the center of the Earth for recycling. Negative entities are other-dimensional human or animal energy interference. These may be the lost astral bodies of people or pets who have died, but do not know how to fully pass from the earthplane. They can also be spirits who have died but refuse to leave, or who are drawn back by some lust or habit. They are often drawn to alcohol or drugs, and attach to the energy of those who use them. Some may be sex addicts. These once human or animal Be-ings must go to the between-life state for healing and reincarnation, but cannot do so without help. Elementals are distorted Earth energies trapped above ground that belong at the center of the Earth.

All of these can cause disruption and discord in human lives, as well as physical, emotional, or mental dis-ease. Some attachments and elementals were karmically placed in our energies for just that purpose, to carry and manifest a piece of personal karma. Others, and most entities, are simply passing through. As the Earth moves from the third to the fifth dimension, it passes through the lower astral energy band, or lower fourth dimension, where misplaced and negative energies reside. One of the jobs most psychics and healers have karmically agreed to take on is the cleaning up of the fourth dimension (lower astral). Eventually, most of these disturbances will leave on their own, but why wait?

On a more structural level, you may *ask the Lords of Karma to clear your DNA of a dis-ease.* These are usually genetic dis-eases, including cancer. It is best to do this only after you have reconnected and reactivated your twelve-strand DNA, and after you have cleared your energy of all negative interference. I did this with a woman with muscular dystrophy and she felt profound changes in her energy system over a period of four months. The results have been encouraging, but they're still inconclusive at this time. If you feel you may be at risk for a genetic dis-ease, you may also ask that the possibility of it manifesting be removed from your DNA. Brede has informed me that DNA work has a most important healing potential, and that once your DNA has been cleared of something, you will no longer pass it on to your children. She also said that children already born are cleared genetically when their parents ask for this, whether the children have asked for the healing themselves or not. No promises can be made here for any medical cures.

Another request I recommend to everyone is to *ask to heal, bring in, and integrate all your soul fragments.* A severe trauma, shock or fright can cause your Astral Twin to split and break into pieces. The pieces are fragments of the personality "self," and each carries a different aspect of karma from the trauma that caused the split. The Astral Twin reincarnates in this fragmented and damaged state if the traumas are not healed during the lifetime in which they occurred. If these unhealed fragments become developed enough and remain unrepaired through many lifetimes, they can be triggered by present trauma to become the source of multiple personality disorder. While only a few people have that much astral damage, most of us have soul fragments that need healing.

There are a number of techniques for bringing in and integrating soul fragments. The process is often used in shamanism, and can also be done as a psychic healing process. The simplest and most complete way of doing it, however, is to ask the Lords of Karma to effect this piece of core soul healing for you. Be sure to ask that the fragments be healed as they are brought in, and also that they be fully integrated. Unhealed fragments are like emotionally damaged children; they are in pain themselves, and they wreak havoc upon others. They must be integrated or the healing remains incomplete, and they may separate again.

When returning soul fragments are brought into your energy, you will feel a warmth at your heart center. A web of light connects the fragments into your energy at the heart, and then grows and extends upward to your crown chakra. The returning fragments may psychically appear as little children in your heart. As they integrate, they go to sleep and fade. When they first come in, talk to them as if they *were* children, thank them for returning, and welcome them home. The integration can take a few days, and you will feel relaxed and well during the process and after it. When you ask the Lords of Karma for this healing, you may notice one or more fragments coming in immediately, and others appearing later, at times when you are relaxed or nearly asleep. It takes about three weeks for all the fragments to come in for most people. If many of them have split off in past lives, however, you may be surprised to find them still returning to you even after months. This is a gentle, peaceful healing that brings emotional stability and calm into your life. If granted by the Lords of Karma, it needs to be requested only once.

Uncording is another process that can be done during energy balancing, and I recommend that everyone do this fully at least once. It must be done in parts to complete the work on both kundalini and hara energy lines, and you can do all the parts in one session. First, *ask the Lords of Karma to clear, release, and heal your kundalini chakras of all negative cords*. The process moves from chakra to chakra, and you may be given images along the way of whom the cords are connected to. If you are shown an image, don't refuse it, as the knowledge may be required for the cord's release. You may have many cords in each chakra, or only a few, most people have many. When this part of the work is finished, next *ask the Lords of Karma to clear, release, and heal gently your kundalini chakras of all negative hooks*. Cords are negative emotional attachments to your energy made by other people in this lifetime. Hooks are deeper attachments from people that you have incarnated with before and have much karma with now. We are born with these hooks, while the cords accumulate in this life. Never attempt to psychically pull out or rip out a hook, as you will become very sick if you do. Instead, wait for the Lords of Karma to dissolve them.

When the kundalini chakras are finished, *ask the Lords of Karma to clear, release, and heal your hara line chakras of all negative hooks*. Cords do not develop on the hara line, but the hooks appear very large and are serious obstructions to your life path. There is rarely more than one per chakra, and they won't appear in every chakra. Again, it is important not to pull at these; ask that they be dissolved. Also ask that the healing and integration be comfortable and easy. Otherwise, the great deal of toxins and energy damage that cords and hooks contain may leave you feeling unwell for a couple of weeks. Their removal is freeing and healing, however, and you will be very glad you did it.

A final item, offered with caution, is to *ask the Lords of Karma to release, heal, and clear your energy of all heart scars.* I offer this with caution, as it can be a very uncomfortable healing, though an ultimately positive one. Heart scars are the result of great emotional pain in this lifetime. Almost everyone has at least one of them. They prevent full emotional blossoming and heart opening, and make it difficult to develop positive trust and a healthy self-image. If left unhealed in this lifetime, they become karmic issues for lifetimes to come. Their removal can be very painful, however, and may occur in several episodes if there are several scars. My most typical scenario with these is to wake from calm sleep in a panic attack. The painful old pictures of the heart scar's origin appear in living color in my mind and memory, as if they were happening again now, and my heart chakra feels like a real heart attack is coming on.

While there is clear awareness that the pain is emotional rather than physical, the release of heart scars is still quite scary and intense. The process ends within an hour, but it's not an easy hour. If you ask for this healing, be careful what you ask for and make sure you are ready for what will come. The release will probably not manifest immediately but usually within three days. Also, ask the Lords of Karma to make the clearing as gentle and easy as possible.

These are some sample core soul healings to do in the energy balancing process. They are highly complex healings with profound results, yet are accomplished so simply by this method. You may also go through each component of energy anatomy that you are aware of, one piece at a time, asking the Lords of Karma to clear, heal, align, open, and activate each part. Activating your Sliver Cord in this way is especially positive, and should be repeated often. With proficiency in these healings, you will probably think of other things to add. If you are unsure about any of this, you may ask the Lords of Karma's advice on whether it is positive or not for you to proceed with any request, and they will help you with each step. They are delighted that we are repairing our many lifetimes' damage to our energy and our souls.

Essence Self, Goddess Self, and Goddess

WHEN YOU HAVE BECOME FAMILIAR WITH THE basic energy balancing process, at least some of the core soul healings, and have become proficient at bringing in and talking with your Higher Self, it's time to meet the rest of your personality "selves" and bring them into your consciousness. Each of these should be done as separate processes, allowing time in between to get used to the changes in your energy. Because the outer body "selves" are very powerful, these meditations are best done lying down, preferably in bed before sleep, or when you have at least two hours free to enjoy them. The entrance of both Essence Self and Goddess Self begins periods of change and purification in your entire energy system that may last for several weeks before your Goddess can enter. You will feel blissful, but also spacey and out of body for a few hours after each "self" initially enters. When you need to get up, however, the spaciness leaves and you will be able to function easily. You will still retain the sense of peace, relaxation, and joy.

Meeting and Bringing in Your Essence/Star Self

First meet and bring in your Essence/Star Self. She is placed in your energy on the lower level of the causal body, and is the next personality "self" beyond the spiritual body's Higher Self. When she enters, this is what happens. The Essence Self will first send a line or cord of energy that connects her to the back of your Higher Self at the heart. She then will merge with the Higher Self for the length of the meditation. In time, she will remain merged with your Higher Self permanently. The light that proceeds from Higher Self through Astral Twin and Etheric Double and into your closer-to-physical energy will now extend higher and more strongly. The entire chain or column of light that runs through all the "selves" becomes brighter and broader, and each energy structure that it passes through is healed and strengthened. It may take several months for the Essence Self to merge in this way completely, and you and she will go through a time of integration.

The Essence Self clears and purifies all the energy she passes through and connects with as she comes into your consciousness. The initial contact with her may initiate several weeks of shifts and changes. Check frequently to see that the energy bodies remain in alignment, and that all the templates are clear and open. Shifting energy can cause misalignments that are easy to fix by repeating the energy balancing procedure. You may feel some disturbance in your energy for a few days, but you will also be very relaxed and unafraid of it. Check to see if any of your energy bodies, your Silver Cord, the hara line chakras or kundalini chakras need clearing, and ask the Lords of Karma to do what is needed.

Essence Selves are angels. If you have had any doubt of what or who angels are, or of their existence at all, you will meet them now. You may ask one directly to account for herself. They are far more than spirit guides. They are real, and they are you. Not all types of angels are Essence Selves, the repositories of our Akashic Records, but our Essence Selves are all from a particular category of angels. When your Essence Self comes in, you may see many flying angels in your field of psychic vision. You may have a clearer visual image of your Essence Self than you did of your Higher Self. Your Essence Self is an angel, wings and all.

To begin the meditation, *ask to speak with the Lords of Karma*. First, ask them to *align all of your energy bodies and the connections between the energy bodies*. When this is complete, ask to *clear, heal, align, open, and activate your Ka Template*. When the energy sensations stop, ask to *clear, heal, align, open, and activate your Etheric Template*. Next, ask to *clear, heal, align, open, and activate your Ketheric Template*. Wait for the energy shifts to finish after each request. Then, ask to *clear, heal, align, open, and activate your Celestial Template*. Finally, when you are ready, ask to *clear, heal, align, open, and activate your I-Am Template*. Do the steps in the above order, and wait for each to finish before going on.

If you hear a "no" from the Lords of Karma at any point, ask what you need to know or do to continue. Release with the Lords of Karma process anything you are shown, or follow the directions they give you. By the time you have come this far in clearing your energy, and have brought in your Higher Self often to heal your energy and core soul, a "no" is unlikely. If something needs to be done before you can proceed at any point, you will be told what to do and will then be able to continue. *Ask to clear, heal, and fully activate your Silver Cord*, and wait for the clearing to end.

Next, *ask your Higher Self to come in*. She has become an old friend by now, someone you should be able to talk with, ask for help, and gain information and learn from. Merging your Essence Self with her will bring her joy, and she will help with the process in every possible way. Now, *ask Your Higher Self to clear, heal, align, open, activate, and fill your hara line channels and chakras*. When you feel the energy of this reach your feet, *ask her to clear, heal, align, open, activate, and fill your kundalini line channels and chakras*. Wait for this to finish as well. So far the process is familiar.

To open the access to your Essence Self, now *ask to clear, heal, align, open, and activate the three Galactic Templates*. You will feel much activity and may see colors and light with this step. The first Galactic Template operates through your thymus chakra on the hara line. I have named it the Intergalactic Template, as it offers connection to and conscious awareness of the ships that will take us home to our planet of origin. The second Galactic Template I call the Ascension Template. It connects to our nearer-to-physical energy through the hara chakra on the emotional body hara line. The hara chakra, or just hara, is the central repository of our life purpose for this incarnation and of our ability to accomplish it. The third Galactic Template I have named the Star Self Template, as it is the Essence Self's access for entering our consciousness and joining our closer-to-physical energy. It connects through the causal body chakra on the hara line.

When the Galactic Templates are opened and activated, *ask to clear, heal, align, open, and activate the five galactic chakras*. The Galactic Chakras are located down our back, on an outer level. When developed they connect with the three lower Kundalini Chakras. This is the point at which you may see dozens of flying angels. When it happened for me, they seemed excited and joyful—and very busy. They were dressed in many colors and their flight fully defied any notion of Earthly gravity. They will probably be too busy to talk with you, and will move too fast, but you will take on some of their excitement and happiness. It's hard not to. Wait for the activity to stop, or at least pause, before going further.

Ask now for *your Essence Self/Star Self to come in and to connect and merge with your Higher Self*. You may see her clearly, more clearly than you did your Higher Self. *Ask her name and talk with her awhile*. By this time you will have many questions. It took a few tries for me to understand my Essence Self's name, and I questioned her until I understood. She will talk with you readily, and offer information on Essence Selves and angels if you ask. You will first see her form, then see her throw out a lasso or cord of light. The light falls downward to join or plug into your Higher Self at the back of her heart. Your Essence Self then seems to slide down the light stream and join with your Higher Self's welcoming energy. When I watched this, lights and colors rose like a fountain of splashing water. Every sensation in the process feels wonderful. Take some time to experience it.

Ask your Essence Self to remain connected permanently with your Higher Self and with your energy and consciousness, and end the meditation. Remain lying quietly while the sensations, colors, and energy activity continue. For me this lasted about two hours, after which I reluctantly had to get up. The joy and well-being remained, and I felt like all my bodies were operating somewhere else without me for a few days, but it was all gentle and ecstatic. From here on, whenever you bring in your Higher Self, ask also to "clear and activate the Galactic Chakras and Templates and bring in your Essence Self."

Wait at least a week after this before bringing in your Goddess Self for the first time. You will need the time to integrate the changes that your Essence Self's presence is making in your energy, and the healing she is accomplishing for you at all levels. This is a very intense energy, but all gentle and comforting. Angels are our protectors and teachers, and your Essence Self is also the Mother of the Goddess triad. When you feel ready to bring in your Goddess Self, do it when going to bed so you will have the night ahead of you to enjoy the process.

Meeting and Bringing in Your Goddess Self/Oversoul

To bring in your Goddess Self/Oversoul, do the full energy balancing process as before. Align your energy bodies, clear and activate the five primary templates, activate your Sliver Cord, bring your Higher Self in, and clear and align the hara and kundalini channels. Ask to clear and activate the three Galactic Templates, five galactic chakras, and invite your Essence Self in to join with your Higher Self. All of this happens in just a few minutes once you are used to the process.

Now, *ask the Lords of Karma to clear, heal, align, open, and activate the three Causal Body Templates.* The energy may be very intense this time, but will also feel very far away. You will have a sense of light and speed, but possibly nothing more clear or visual. The opening will happen very rapidly, in a flurry of activity. Wait for all activity to end before going on. Then, *ask to clear, heal, align, open, and activate the five Causal Body Chakras.* Note that these chakras and templates are located at the higher causal body level of your energy system. They are not the hara line causal body chakra that is located at the back of your neck on the nearer-to-physical emotional level. Wait again for the sensations to finish before going on.

Now, *ask your Goddess Self/Oversoul to come in, and to connect and merge with your Essence/Star Self and Higher Self.* You may find it harder to obtain a visual image at this level, as everything at this level feels much too distant, which it is. The energy sensation is unmistakable, however. Something is there, something very strong, good, and powerful. When your Goddess Self seems fully in, *ask her name*. You may seem to just know it, now or later, without actually hearing her say it. The names of Higher Self, Essence Self, and Goddess Self may be close to each other, even containing a common first syllable, as mine do. Your soul's true name, through all its incarnations, changes, and millennia, is the name given you by your Goddess Self.

Conversation with your Goddess Self may be difficult, as she feels so very distant. As she merges with your Essence and Higher Selves, however, she moves closer to and integrates with your consciousness. This will make her more accessible for conversation in time. She brings with her a strong and secure sense of well-being and joy, that becomes consciously stronger with each passing day. *Invite your Goddess Self to remain connected to your Essence Self and Higher Self permanently*. This will not happen immediately, and may take several days for the initial connection. Merging and integration take longer, probably several months. Remember from how far away your Goddess Self is coming to join with you.

Now, *invite your Goddess to come in, to connect and merge with your Goddess Self, and to join with your energy through all the levels and "selves."* The sensations here are primarily of light and may seem quiet or dramatic. When she is fully within your energy, ask your Goddess' name. It will be one you know and love. Never demand your Goddess' presence and merging, always ask or invite instead.

Ask that all the processes and alignments you have now completed become permanent and self-sustaining on all levels.

Repetition may be required for a while to make them so, but you are on your way to this very positive permanence. *Come back to now*, but give yourself time—the whole night if possible—to relax with the energy and the changes in your aura. You may spend the night talking with your Higher Self, Essence Self, Goddess Self, and Goddess, or just soaking up the colors and the joy. You have made a great step forward in your soul's evolution in a very short time. Don't forget to say thank you. A brief outline of these two meditations is included in Appendix II.

The final chapter of this book discusses follow-up processes, how to secure and maintain the gains you have now achieved.

Follow Up

THE REQUESTS THAT YOU MAKE TO THE LORDS of Karma, once granted and brought through all the levels, all the bodies, and all the lifetimes, including the present lifetime, with all the damage healed, and the healing brought into the present now, become permanent immediately. There is no need to ask for these releases again, though there may sometimes be a delay in the changes manifesting on the earthplane or in your realizing that they have. This delay may last anywhere from a few days to a few months, at the longest, for those processes that haven't happened instantly.

In the energy balancing process, however, parts of the work need to be done only once, while other parts must be repeated. Some require frequent repetition, while others only need to be checked upon from time to time and repeated if needed. If a template or chakra system has gone out of alignment or needs more healing, for example, you may either repeat the entire energy balancing or request to rebalance just that part. Our energy bodies are constantly shifting to accommodate a variety of changing factors, and alignment is a relative thing.

The request for DNA reconnection and activation, and the request for core soul healing need only to be done once. Until your Essence Self and Goddess Self are brought in, however, the alignment of the energy bodies and the connections between them may shift frequently. They become more stable once the outer "selves" are integrated. If you start to feel agitated, unbalanced, or out of sorts, check to see if your bodies need to be realigned. Doing so will calm and soothe your energy immediately. The first five templates go through frequent movement and energy shifts, and may need to be aligned and cleared often. If you do it for one template, do it for all five. The alignment and clearing of the hara line and kundalini line channels and the clearing of the Sliver Cord should also be checked frequently. Once your Higher Self is fully in, they will need less maintenance. Ask to clear and activate the Galactic and Causal Body templates and chakras every time you bring your Essence and Goddess Self in.

I use a pendulum to do this checking up, and I do it twice a day, in the morning before getting up and at night before sleeping. Go through each step of the energy balancing with the pendulum, asking "Do I need an energy body alignment?" "Do the templates need to be cleared?" "Does the hara line need to be cleared?" "The kundalini line?" " The Sliver Cord?" If any template needs work, I go through the process of clearing, healing, aligning, opening, and activating all five of them. Once you know what needs to be done, ask the Lords of Karma to come in, and request each process in turn. Go step by step as when doing the full energy balancing, which you may also wish to do, and complete each step before moving to the next. At least once a week for the first few months, do a full energy balancing process, whether you feel you need it or not. After the first few months of working with your outer body "selves," you will need to check only weekly to see what repetition is needed (though I still do it twice daily).

Once a week, also check the energy bodies themselves. Ask if you need healing and clearing at the etheric body level, the astral/emotional body level, the mental body or mind grid, and the spiritual/causal level. At some point, you may wish to use the energy balancing additional item process to ask the Lords of Karma to *clear and heal your mind grid of all negative or outmoded thought forms*. Beyond the mind grid and mental body level, the bodies will not need clearing, and the core soul healing request takes care of any healing that remains above this level. You may ask at this time, too, if your Etheric Double or Astral Twin needs healing. Your Higher Self, Essence Self, Goddess Self, and Goddess will not. If you wish, you may also check each chakra on the hara and kundalini line, but if you align and heal the channels as a whole they probably will require little or no individual work.

This sounds like a lot, but in fact it goes very quickly. It probably will take less than ten minutes to check and clear everything required to bring your Higher Self in. It is important to bring your Higher Self, Essence Self, Goddess Self, and Goddess into your energy at least once a day. The more you are willing to do this, the faster these energy "selves" will connect permanently and integrate fully. Again, the whole process moves very quickly, but first check to see what needs work, and ask the Lords of Karma to do it. Make especially sure that the templates are cleared and activated. If they are not, your outer body "selves" and Goddess will be unable to come in.

Once everything is cleared and fully aligned, *ask your Higher Self to come into your energy*. When she enters, ask her to fill first the hara line and then the kundalini line. Next, ask your Essence Self to *clear and activate the three Galactic Templates and five Galactic Chakras, and join with your Higher Self*. This will all happen very quickly, almost as fast as you can ask for it. Once your Essence Self is fully merged with your Higher Self, ask your Goddess Self to *clear and activate the three Causal Body Templates and five causal body chakras and join with your Essence and Higher Selves*. She will also come in immediately. Next *invite your Goddess to come in, to connect and merge with you through all your levels and "selves."* When she has done so invite them all to stay with you. Spend some time talking with them or just go to sleep. The whole sequence takes only moments.

If you wish to do healing closer to your physical levels, you may wish to work with the hara line and kundalini lines. Brede has given me a series of symbols, some of them Reiki symbols, to clear, connect, and activate the energy of both etheric and emotional/astral bodies. The symbols are visualized, as when doing distance healing. In the meditative state, imagine or see your energy self standing before you and trace the symbols in gold light over each chakra. If you only see a body outline this is fine, and if the colors change from gold it is fine, too. Doing this provides healing, alignment, and clearing for the hara chakras and their connections into the kundalini chakras of the etheric body. It also helps your Higher Self to be able to merge more fully with your Astral Twin and Etheric Double, and to heal any damage to them that may remain.

DIAGRAM 4. HARA HEALING SYMBOLS

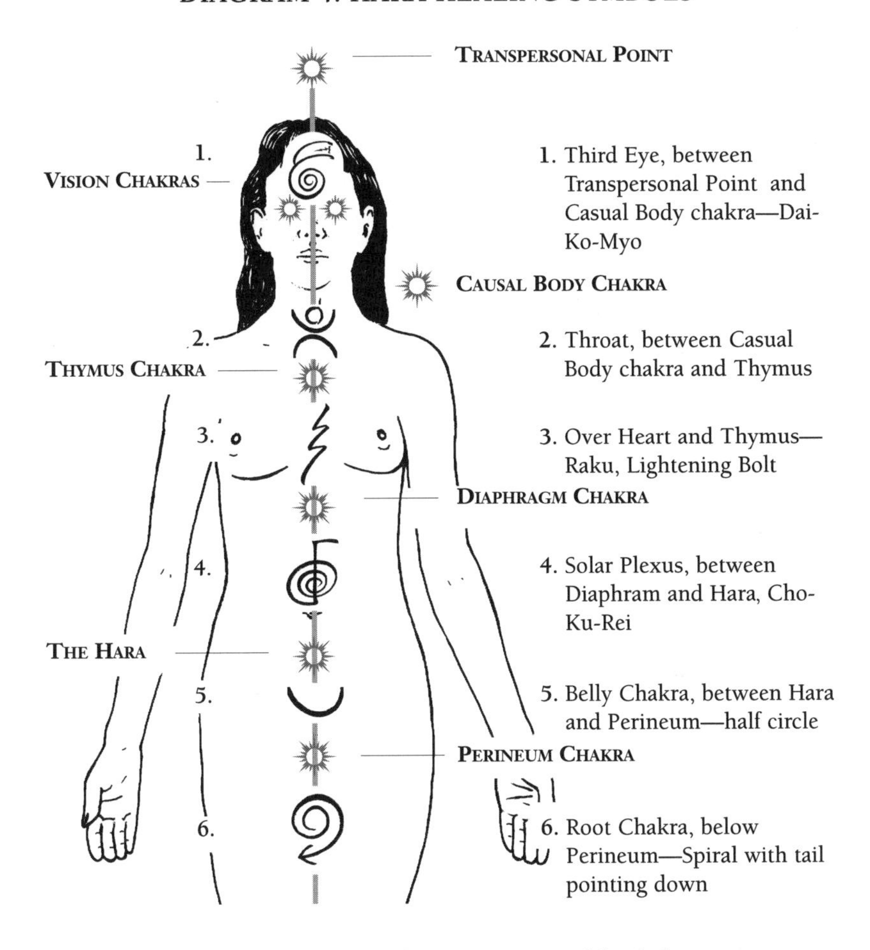

These five symbols used in healing connect and heal the connections between Kundalini and Hara Line Channels, Physical, Etheric and Astral Bodies.

The symbols proceed from head to root/perineum. They do not cover every kundalini and hara chakra but only those major chakra sites that have physical body connections to both bodies' energy. The first of these is over the forehead or kundalini third eye, between the hara transpersonal point and the hara line causal body chakra. The symbol is the Reiki Master symbol, the Dai-Ko-Myo, symbol of soul-level healing. The next one is over the kundalini throat center, between the hara line causal body chakra and the thymus chakra. The symbol here looks like a simple human figure, a half circle pointing down, a second one above it pointing up, and a small circle inside the upward pointing half-circle. It is not a form used in Reiki. The third symbol is over the kundalini heart and hara line thymus chakras. It's the Reiki Raku, the lightning bolt, symbol of enlightenment and transcendence.

Next, over the kundalini solar plexus, between the hara line diaphragm and hara chakras, place a Reiki Cho-Ku-Rei symbol. This is the symbol for increasing the power of any healing and a symbol for healing at the physical body level. The fifth symbol, over the kundalini belly chakra, between the hara and perineum chakras on the hara line, is an upward pointing half circle or half-moon. It is not a Reiki symbol, but may be the half-moon form used in India to represent the belly chakra. The last symbol is placed over the kundalini root chakra, below the perineum. This one is a clockwise spiral with tail pointing down; imagine it drawing the energy of the healing downward, between the legs and into the Earth between the feet.

These are simple, easy-to-learn symbols and quite powerful. You may wish to use them in distance healing with others, as well as for your own etheric and astral well-being. If your energy feels blocked or damaged at any time on either level, the above symbols may quickly clear the problem.

This book has been only an introduction to the possibilities opening to us for healing our energy and our Be-ing. If karma is truly ended on this planet, it will free us for more new beginnings than we can now imagine or dream of. We are one small planet in a boundless galaxy and universe. By raising our abilities to reconnect with and heal our own energy, we begin both healing planet Earth and reconnecting with and healing our place in the universe. At this point we have a long way to go, but we have begun.

Use the processes of this book with thanks and great respect for the gifts the Lords of Karma have offered us. The methods are simple, and they need to be used and shared. Even children can do karmic release and energy balancing and do them well. By starting their energy healing early, who knows how far beyond us today's children may evolve? Remember also to use these methods for animal healing. They suffer as much as we do and devote their lives to serving us.

One day soon the Lords of Karma will be out of work, and energy balancing will be a redundant idea. How well we learn and do karmic healing now will determine how soon that will be. When there is no more karma and everyone has all her "selves" and the Goddess integrated into her energy, we will be more evolved people on a more enlightened planet. We may then be ready for ascension and rejoining the intergalactic community. Until then, let us use the karmic processes to start on a path of healing for everyone and the Earth.

December 24, 1996
Full Moon in Gemini

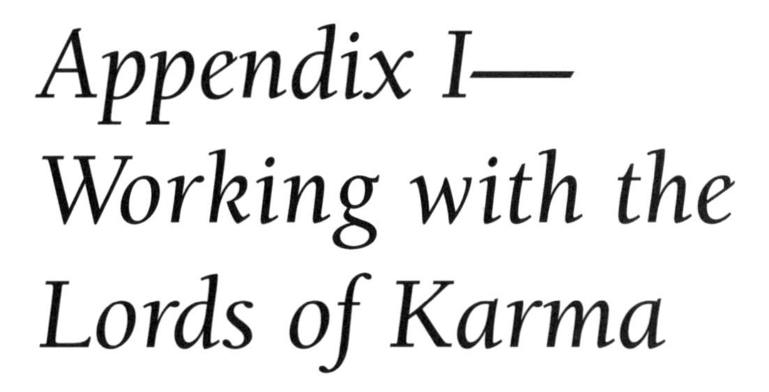

Appendix I—Working with the Lords of Karma

1. Ask to speak with the Lords of Karma, you will receive some perception of them.
2. Ask for the karmic release you wish.
3. You will receive a "yes" or "no" response.
4. If the answer is "yes," ask to have the release:

   Through all the levels and all the bodies,
   All the lifetimes including the present lifetime,
   Heal all the damage from the situation,
   And bring the healing into the present NOW.

   If the answer is "yes" again, the process is finished.

5. If the answer to your request is "no," ask what you need to know or do to have the release, and wait for a response. If you are shown a past life or other information you may or may not understand, ask to clear and release what you are seeing. You will get a "yes" or "no" answer—if "yes," do #4. If "no," ask again what you need to know or do to release it. Once you get a "yes" to releasing the obstacle, go back to your original request and ask again. You will likely get a "yes." Do #4 to finish.
6. If you get a "no" to #4, ask for a "yes" or "no" to each phrase. When you find the "no," do #5.
7. You may ask as many requests at a time as you wish, as often as you wish. Keep the requests very simple; process one at a time.
8. Use this process on four categories of karmic healing:
    a. to heal dis-eases or physical conditions
    b. to heal conflicted relationships of all types
    c. to heal negative personality traits or habits
    d. to heal negative life situations
9. Treat these Be-ings with great respect, never argue with them, and say thank you.

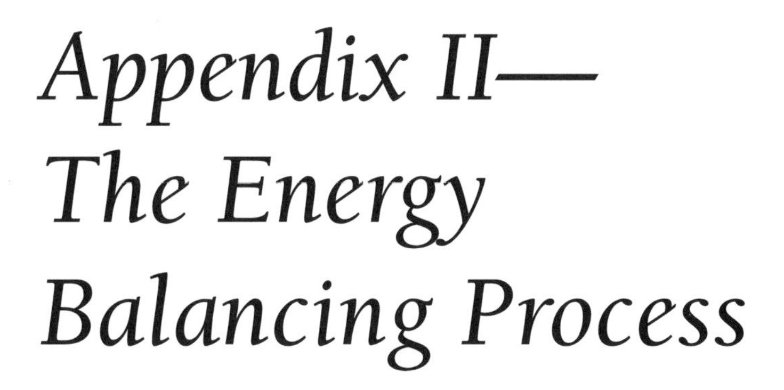

Appendix II—The Energy Balancing Process

Part I—The Basic Process

Important: Complete each step before going to the next. Each step takes about five minutes.

1. Ask to speak with the Lords of Karma.
2. Ask them to align all of your energy bodies and the connections between energy bodies.
3. Ask to clear, heal, align, open and activate:
    a. the Ka Template
    b. the Etheric Template

   c. the Ketheric Template
   d. the Celestial Template
   e. the I-Am Template

   Do these one at a time in this order; finish each before asking for the next.
4. Ask to reconnect, heal, and activate your twelve-strand DNA.
5. Ask for complete core soul healing.
6. Optional processes, see Chapter 11.
7. Ask your Higher Self to come in:
   a. ask her name.
   b. ask her for a gift.
   c. she will ask a gift of you.
   d. invite her to remain connected with you permanently.
8. Ask your Higher Self to clear, heal, align, open, activate, and fill your hara line channels and chakras.
9. Ask your Higher Self to clear, heal, align, open, activate, and fill your kundalini channels and chakras.
10. Ask that the processes and alignments just completed become permanent.
11. Come back to now.

Part II—The Essence Self

Complete each step before going on to the next.

1. Ask to speak with the Lords of Karma.
2. Ask them to align all of your energy bodies and the connections between the energy bodies.
3. Ask to clear, heal, align, open, and activate:
    a. the Ka Template
    b. the Etheric Template
    c. the Ketheric Template
    d. the Celestial Template
    e. the I-Am Template
4. Ask to clear, heal, and fully activate your Sliver Cord.
5. Ask your Higher Self to come in.
6. Ask her to clear, heal, align, open, activate, and fill the hara line channels and chakras.
7. Ask her to clear, heal, align, open, activate, and fill the kundalini line channels and chakras.
8. Ask to clear, heal, align, open, and activate the three Galactic Templates.
9. Ask to clear, heal, align, open, and activate the five Galactic Chakras.
10. Ask your Essence Self/Star Self to come in and to connect and merge with your Higher Self.
11. Talk with her a bit, ask her to remain connected permanently.
12. Come back to now, but remain lying still for the length of the experience, at least two hours.

Part III—The Goddess Self

1. Repeat Part II, Steps one through ten. Complete each step before going on to the next.
2. Ask to clear, heal, align, open, and activate the three Causal Body Templates.
3. Ask to clear, heal, align, open, and activate the five causal body chakras.
4. Ask your Goddess Self/Oversoul to come in, and to connect and merge with your Essence Self and Higher Self.
5. Ask her name, talk with her.
6. Ask your Goddess Self to remain connected permanently. (This process may take several days.)
7. Invite your Goddess to come in, to connect and merge with your Goddess Self, and to join with your energy through all the levels and "selves." Talk with her, ask her name.
8. Ask that the processes and alignments just completed become permanent.
9. Come back to now, but remain lying still for the length of the experience, at least two hours.

Books by Diane Stein

All Women Are Healers:
A Comprehensive Guide to Natural Healing

A wealth of "how-to" information on various healing methods including Reiki, reflexology, polarity balancing, and homeopathy, intended to teach women to take control of their bodies and lives.

$14.95 • Paper • 0-89594-409-X

A Woman's I Ching

Finally, a feminist interpretation of the popular ancient text for divining the character of events. Stein's version reclaims the feminine, or *yin*, content of the ancient work and removes all oppressive language and imagery. Her interpretation envisions a healing world in which women can explore different roles free from the shadow of patriarchy.

$16.95 • Paper • 0-89594-857-5

Casting the Circle:
A Women's Book of Ritual

A comprehensive guide including 23 full rituals for waxing, full, and waning moons, the eight Sabats, and rites of passage.

$14.95 • Paper • 0-89594-411-1

Essential Reiki:
A Complete Guide to an Ancient Healing Art

While no book can replace the directly received Reiki attunements, *Essential Reiki* provides everything else that the healer, practitioner, and the teacher of this system needs, including full information on all three degrees of Reiki, most of it in print for the first time.

$18.95 • Paper • 0-89594-736-6

Books by Diane Stein

On Grief and Dying:
Understanding the Soul's Journey
Guiding the reader on a healing journey to a place of loving acceptance, this book offers comfort and help to persons facing death and to those who love them.
$15.00 • Hardcover • 0-89594-830-3

The Goddess Celebrates:
An Anthology of Women's Rituals
Contributors include Z. Budapest, Starhawk, and others.
$14.95 • Paper • 0-89594-460-X

Healing with Flower and Gemstone Essences
This book provides a complete guide to healing the body, mind, and spirit with the aid of flower and gemstone essences. Instructions for choosing and using flowers and gems are combined with descriptions of their effect on emotional balance, an important concept in the emerging field of psychonneuroimmunology.
$14.95 • Paper • 0-89594-856-7

Healing with Gemstones and Crystals
Provides a complete guide to healing the body, mind, and spirit with the aid of gemstone and crystals. Details on choosing gems are supplemented by explanations of the significance of this type of healing for the planet, for our past and future lives, and other forms of consciousness.
$14.95 • Paper • 0-89594-831-1

Books by Diane Stein

The Natural Remedy Book for Women

This best-seller includes information on ten natural healing methods—vitamins and minerals, herbs, naturopathy, homeopathy and cell salts, amino acids, acupressure, aromatherapy, flower essences, gemstones and emotional healing. Remedies from all ten methods are given for fifty common health problems.

$16.95 • Paper • 0-89594-525-8

Psychic Healing with Spirit Guides and Angels

This book presents a complete program of soul development for self-healing, healing with others, and Earth healing. Advanced skills include healing karma and past lives, soul retrieval, releasing entities and spirit attachments, and understanding and aiding the death process.

$18.95 • Paper • 0-89594-807-9

Related Books from The Crossing Press

Healing with Astrology

by Marcia Starck

Medicine woman and medical astrologer, Marcia Starck, provides detailed descriptions of the correspondence between the planetary cycles and a variety of healing systems—vitamin therapy, herbs, music, color, crystals, gemstones, flower remedies, aromatherapy, and unification rituals, and offers us the opportunity to reunite the healing wisdom of the Goddess tradition with the planets and stars as they appear in our birth charts.

$14.95 • Paper • ISBN 0-89594-862-1

Healing With Chinese Herbs

By Lesley Tierra, L.Ac., Dip. Ac.

Tierra lists the properties of over 100 herbs, outlining their therapeutic uses and explaining how prescriptions are tailored to each patient's constitutional strength and particular condition. With a glossary of Chinese terms, an index to the Latin and Mandarin names of each herb, and guidelines to dosages, this is a vital book for anyone interested in adding traditional Chinese herbal medicine to their health practices.

$14.95 • Paper •ISBN 0-89594-829-X

The Sevenfold Journey

Reclaiming Mind, Body & Spirit Through the Chakras

By Anodea Judith & Selene Vega

Combining yoga, movement, psychotherapy, and ritual, the authors weave ancient and modern wisdom into powerful techniques for facilitating personal growth and healing.

$18.95 • Paper •ISBN 0-89594-574-6

Shamanism as a Spiritual Practice for Daily Life

By Tom Cowan

This inspirational book blends elements of shamanism with inherited traditions and contemporary religious commitments.

$16.95 • Paper •ISBN 0-89594-838-9

Mother Wit

A Guide to Healing and Psychic Development

By Diane Mariechild

"It is a joy to find this material from occult traditions and Eastern religions adapted by her woman-identified consciousness to the needs of women today." —Womanspirit

$14.95 • Paper •ISBN 0-89594-358-11

Chakras and Their Archetypes

Uniting Energy Awareness and Spiritual Growth

By Ambika Wauters

In Chakras and Their Archetypes, we find that creating healthy archetypes is both liberating and fundamental to our well being. By relating them to the seven chakras, author Ambika Wauters guides us on a journey to understand where our energy is blocked, and which attitudes or emotional issues are responsible.

$16.95 • Paper •ISBN 0-89594-891-5

Wishing Well

Empowering Your Hopes and Dreams

By Patricia Telesco

Wishing Well is an engaging probe into the historical roots and lore surrounding this ancient art, offering thirty meditative applications. Fourteen steps are presented for designing, casting, and releasing our wishes towards their goals.

$14.95 • Paper • ISBN 0-89594-870-2

Experiential Astrology

Symbolic Journeys Using Guided Imagery

By Babs Kirby

A psychotherapist and astrologer, Babs Kirby is on the vanguard combining transpersonal psychology with astrology. In Experiential Astrology, she introduces the use of guided journeys that will take us to a deeper awareness of our relationship to planetary principles.

$14.95 • Paper • ISBN 0-89594-798-6

Your Body SpeaksYour Mind

How Your Thoughts and Emotions Affect Your Health

By Debbie Shapiro

This healing guide explores the structural body from the head to the toes, and the inner relationship of each part. We are given tools for using the power of the mind and heart to heal the body through breath awareness, movement, relaxation, meditation, creative visualization, and other complementary healing techniques.

$14.95 • Paper • ISBN 0-89594-893-1